LYNDON B. JOHNSON
1908 –

Chronology-Documents-Bibliographical Aids

Edited by
Howard B. Furer

Series Editor
Howard F. Bremer

1971
OCEANA PUBLICATIONS, INC.
Dobbs Ferry, New York

Library of Congress Catalog Card Number: 75-95015

International Standard Book Number: 0-379-12077-1

Manufactured in the United States of America

CONTENTS

BIBLIOGRAPHICAL AIDS

EDITOR'S FOREWORD

Every attempt has been made to cite the most accurate dates in this chronology. Diaries, documents, memoirs, newspapers and similar evidence has been used to determine the exact date. However, as a result of the short span of time that has elapsed since the conclusion of the Johnson Administrations, not all of the pertinent data has yet been made available. Because of this fact, some of the events cited have been given conflicting dates in some of the sources consulted. In such cases, the most plausible date has been listed. The editor looks forward to the future publication of the Johnson Memoirs which, it is hoped, will clear up some of the chronological confusion.

The aim of this volume is to provide in a short, but comprehensive manner, the essential historical facts about the life, and especially, the administrations of Lyndon B. Johnson. While an editor of this type of work does not usually make judgments on the significance of events, or on the actions of the individual involved, the Administrations of Lyndon B. Johnson concerned themselves with so many controversial and important areas, that it was almost impossible for this editor to completely abstain from historical editorializing. However, it is hoped that the judgments which have been made are reasoned and objective ones, based on an understanding of the subject, and, as best as possible, an understanding of the period of history during which he lived. Obviously, much more could have been included in this book, but space limitations forced the writer to be highly selective in his choice of key documents, pertinent facts, and a critical bibliography. This book, however, does provide the reader with an excellent overall picture of Lyndon B. Johnson's life, work, and Presidency. It is a fine starting point for those who are interested in pursuing the subject further. The documents in this volume are taken from: Government Printing Office, *The Public Papers of the Presidents: Lyndon B. Johnson, 1963-1967.* 9 vols. Washington, D.C., 1966-68, and from the *New York Times,* 1968-69.

CHRONOLOGY

YOUTH AND EARLY CAREER

1908

August 27   Born: Near Stonewall, Texas as Lyndon Baines Johnson. Father: Sam Ealy Jr.; Mother: Rebecca Baines.

1913

February   Family moved from Stonewall to Johnson City in Blanco County, Texas.

September 1   Began his education in the Johnson City public schools.

1917

January   Family moved back to the farm near Stonewall and young Lyndon was sent to the one-room Junction School.

1920

June 2   Graduated from Junction's seventh grade at the age of eleven. He was well known for his mammoth ego which revealed itself in humorous ways.

September 1   Entered the eighth grade school at Stonewall, but his mother transferred him to the Albert School for the ninth and tenth grades.

1923

August   Family moved back to Johnson City.

September 1   Lyndon was enrolled at Johnson City High School to complete his senior year. Was chosen a member of the school's debating team.

1924

May 4   Graduated from Johnson City High School at the age of fifteen. He was President of the graduating class of five members. Decided he was finished with schooling.

1

July 10   Lyndon, along with friends Tom and Otto Crider, Otho Summy and Payne Roundtree left Johnson City in a Model T Ford bound for California. In California, he and his friends picked fruit around San Bernadino, washed dishes, and waited on tables. After two hard years, Johnson returned home to Texas.

1926
March   Went to work on a road gang, driving bulldozers and pickup trucks for one dollar a day.

1927
February 7   Entered Southwest Texas State Teacher's College at San Marcos, Texas where he, at first, took sub-college courses in order to qualify for entrance into the regular college program, which he accomplished on March 21, 1927.

1928
September 5 Financial difficulties at home forced Johnson to withdraw temporarily from college. In order to earn sufficient funds to continue his education, he took a job teaching a sixth grade class at Welhausen School in Cotulla, Texas for about nine months. His salary was $125 a month.

1929
June 1   Returned to Southwest Texas State Teacher's College to finish his education.

1930
August 17   Graduated from college receiving a Bachelor of Science degree. He was twenty-two years old.

September 4 Upon graduation, Johnson took a teaching position at a school in Pearsall, Frio County, Texas where he taught public speaking for $50 a month.

October 25   Left Pearsall, and began teaching at Sam Houston High School in Houston, Texas. Taught debating and public speaking for $1600 a year. Became coach of the debating team.

1931
April 1   Johnson's debating team won the Houston city debating championship. They then won the district championship on April 18.

November 24 Worked in Texas millionaire Richard M. Kleberg's campaign for Congress which resulted in a Kleberg victory.

November 29 Appointed Secretary to Congressman-elect Kleberg. Accompanied Kleberg to Washington in December, 1931.

December 5 Arrived in Washington, D.C. to begin a political career that was to span four decades.

December 7 Engaged Speaker of the House John Nance Garner of Texas in a political battle and won. By stirring up local protest, Johnson forced Garner to relinquish post office patronage appointments in Texas.

1932

May 1 During his tenure as Kleberg's Secretary, Johnson advised the Congressman on many pieces of legislation. He also came to know such influential political figures as Tom Connally, Morris Sheppard, Wright Patman and Sam Rayburn. Rayburn became Johnson's "second daddy" in Washington.

November 8 Kleberg won reelection to Congress. Johnson had served as his campaign manager.

1933

March 4 Attended the inauguration of President Franklin Delano Roosevelt. Roosevelt soon became Johnson's "first daddy" in Washington.

April 1 Elected Speaker of the "Little Congress," a youth group composed of all the Congressman's secretaries in Washington.

1934

September 17 Entered Georgetown University Law School, but dropped out after a year as the study of law bored him.

November 17 Married Claudia (Lady Bird) Taylor in San Antonio, Texas. The couple went to Mexico for their honeymoon.

1935

June 1 Congressman Kleberg, on the advice of his wife, fired Johnson as his secretary.

July 1   Appointed State Administrator of the National Youth Administration for Texas by President Roosevelt. Texas politician Maury Maverick was instrumental in getting the job for Johnson.

August 15   Opened his central N Y A headquarters in Austin, Texas

1937

February 24   Decided to run in a special election for the Congressional seat of J.P. Buchanan who had passed away on February 23.

February 25   Alvin Wirtz, a powerful Texas politician, also advised Johnson to run. Wirtz wanted his own man, and, although he had no money to offer him, said he would guide the campaign, write the speeches, and bring pressure on the local political bosses.

February 28   Lady Bird Johnson borrowed $10,000 from her inheritance to finance Lyndon's campaign. On this day, Johnson resigned as State Director of the N Y A.

March 5   Made his opening campaign speech in San Marcos, and announced he was an ardent supporter of President Roosevelt's New Deal.

April 8   Entered Austin General Hospital, Austin, Texas, for an emergency appendectomy.

April 10   Elected to Congress. Johnson defeated eight other candidates and received twenty-seven percent of the vote.

May 11   Flew to Galveston, Texas with Texas Governor James V. Allred to meet with President Roosevelt aboard the Presidential yacht *Potomac*. Their discussion was concerned with the President's impending Court Bill. Joined Roosevelt in the ride to the railroad station from the Galveston dock, and continued with the President by train as far as Fort Worth, Texas.

CONGRESSMAN AND SENATOR

May 18   Sworn in as a member of Congress by Speaker of the House, William B. Bankhead. At the President's request, Johnson was appointed to the House Committee on Naval Affairs. He was twenty-nine years old.

October 22 Lyndon's father, Sam Ealy Jr. died in Austin. Johnson flew to Texas for the funeral.

1938

June 14 Was one of three Texas Congressmen who voted for the first Minimum Wage Law.

November 8 Reelected to the House for the full term of the Seventy-Sixth Congress. Johnson was unopposed in this election in Texas.

1940

April 25 Johnson, Alvin Wirtz and Mayor Tom Miller of Austin drew up the "Harmony Resolution" to unite Texas Democrats behind Roosevelt's attempt for a third term nomination.

May 28 Played an important role at the Texas Democratic State Convention. Succeeded in getting a "stop-Roosevelt" movement outlawed, and was elected Vice-Chairman of the Texas delegation to the National Convention.

July 15 Attended the Democratic National Convention in Chicago and cast his vote for Roosevelt. His attempt to push Sam Rayburn's nomination for Vice-President through the Texas delegation failed.

September 20 Roosevelt put Johnson in charge of the Democratic Congressional campaigns. Johnson did an all-round magnificent job as the Republicans lost five seats in the House to the Democrats. The 1940 campaign dated Lyndon Johnson's status as a national politician.

November 5 Reelected to Congress. Again he was unopposed.

1941

April 22 Announced his candidacy for the Senate to fill the unexpired term of deceased Senator Morris Sheppard on the south portico of the White House. Twenty-nine others announced their candidacy. His candidacy was endorsed by Roosevelt.

May 3 Began his campaign in San Marcos with a speech entitled "Roosevelt and Unity." He pledged that: "If the day ever comes when my vote must be cast to send your boy to the trenches, that day will Lyndon Johnson leave his Senate seat to go with them." Wirtz was his campaign manager.

May 19   Texas Governor W. Lee (Pappy) O'Daniel announced his candidacy for the Senate seat despite earlier assurances to Johnson that he would not run.

June 28   At the end of election day, it appeared that Johnson had been victorious with a 5,000 vote lead over O'Daniel.

July 2   When all the votes had been counted, O'Daniel was declared the winner over Johnson with a margin of 1,311 votes. Johnson returned to Washington to reclaim his House seat.

August 8   Delivered his first major address in the House in defense of Roosevelt's proposal to extend the Selective Service Act. Voted for the Act on August 12.

December 7 Pearl Harbor in the Hawaiian Islands was bombed by Japanese aircraft.

December 8 Voted for the Declaration of War against Japan. Asked to be called for active duty in the Navy having received a commission as Lieutenant Commander in the Naval Reserve on January 21, 1940.

December 11 Voted for the Declaration of War against Germany and Italy. Immediately after the vote, Johnson was ordered to active duty by the Navy. He was the first member of the House to go into uniform.

December 12 Ordered by the Navy to report to San Francisco where he was to occupy a desk in the office of the United States—New Zealand Naval Command.

1942

January 11 Returned to Washington and met with President Roosevelt to ask for a new, more important assignment. Roosevelt proposed that Johnson undertake a survey of military supplies in the Australian combat zone. Johnson quickly agreed.

May 21   Arrived in Auckland, New Zealand to begin his fact finding mission.

May 25   Visited Southwest Pacific Command headquarters for a staff briefing, and was later invited to the private office of General Douglas MacArthur for a personal meeting.

June 12   In an overage B17D named the "Swoose," Johnson fled from Port Moresby to Melbourne, Australia. The "Swoose" ran out of fuel and had to put down in a field near Winston, Australia.

June 18   Was awarded the Silver Star medal by General McArthur for "gallantry in action." Actually, the award was made to remind Johnson of his own belief in the primary importance of the Southwest Pacific Area.

July 1   Roosevelt issued a directive ordering all members of Congress to leave military service and return to their legislative duties. Johnson returned to Washington on July 15.

October 16   Appointed Chairman of the Subcommittee Investigating Manpower Utilization in Naval Affairs. This "watchdog" committee was similar to the one headed by Senator Harry S Truman in the Senate.

November 3   Reelected to the House. Again, he was unopposed.

December 27 Lady Bird and Lyndon purchased radio station KTBC for $17,500 from A.W. Walker, Robert A. Stuart and Robert B. Anderson, all of Texas.

1943

January 25   Station KTBC received the permission of the Federal Communications Commission to go into operation. By 1962 KTBC had an estimated market value of seven million dollars.

1944

January 13   Met with President Roosevelt at the White House to discuss the Presidential election of 1944 and other matters. Agreed to try and persuade the Texas delegation to go to the National Convention pledged to Roosevelt.

March 19   Daughter, Lynda Bird, was born in Washington, D.C.

May 23   Went to Austin to attend the Texas State Democratic

Convention. Despite his efforts, the Convention split into anti-Roosevelt and loyalist groups. The regulars won out and passed a resolution ordering the twenty-three electors to vote for any man except Roosevelt.

July 22   Defeated Buck Taylor, candidate of the "regular" Democrats in Congressional primary election. Could not attend the Democratic National Convention in mid-July because of this challenge at home.

September 23   Alvin Wirtz succeeded in getting a new slate of Democratic electors in Texas, all pledged to Roosevelt.

November 7   Defeated Republican opponent in Texas Congressional election. Despite the victory, Johnson's ambitions seemed to be stalled permanently at the House level.

1945
February 15   Johnson's "Work or Fight" Bill was passed by the House. The Bill was designed to level an assault against absentee war plant workers by permitting management to get rid of those workers who were frequently absent from their jobs. Johnson was bitterly denounced by both the AFL and CIO.

April 12   President Roosevelt died in Georgia. Johnson paid tribute to the dead President in an interview with *New York Time's* reporter, William White.

1946
January 23   Attended Democratic Executive Committee meeting and banquet in Dallas at the invitation of Alvin Wirtz. Wirtz wanted him there to promote him for the Texas Democratic Gubernatorial nomination. However, Johnson failed to make a positive impression, and did not run for governor.

July 21   Defeated Judge Hardy Hollers, the candidate of the "regular" Texas Democrats in a very close Congressional primary election.

August 25   Appointed to twenty-three man Select Committee on Postwar Military Policy.

November 5   Defeated Republican opponent and was reelected to Congress for the fifth time. However, the Republicans gained control of both Houses for the first time in fourteen years.

1947

March 12   Helped push Truman Doctrine through the House. The Doctrine proposed to provide United States support for free peoples who were resisting attempted subjugation by armed minorities or by outside pressures. In a House speech supporting the Doctrine, Johnson rattled the war drums when he said, "The only thing a bully understands is force, and the only thing he fears is courage."

June 23   Voted to override President Truman's veto of the Taft-Hartley Act. He had previously voted in favor of the Bill in the House despite Rayburn's denunciation of it as a "punitive labor bill." Johnson voted against other proposals of the Truman administration and vehemently denounced the President's Civil Rights proposals of 1946-47.

July 2   Daughter, Lucy Baines, was born in Washington, D.C.

September 9   Through Rayburn's influence, Johnson was appointed to the newly created Joint House and Senate Committee on Atomic Energy. By this time, he was also the senior Texas member of the House Armed Services Committee.

1948

May 15   Johnson officially filed for the Texas Democratic Senate Primary. There were seven other candidates running in this primary. The most prominent candidate, and the biggest threat to Johnson, was Ex-Governor Coke Stevenson.

June 7   Delivered radio address in Houston after having returned to Texas from the Mayo Clinic in Rochester, Minnesota, where he was treated for kidney stones. Johnson's campaign slogan was "Peace, Preparedness, Progress."

June 13   Made campaign swing through Northeast Texas in the "Johnson City Windmill," a helicopter purchased by a group of veterans and given to the candidate as a gift. As was expected, few persons in that area of Texas had ever seen a helicopter before and the tour was a rousing success.

June 22   The Texas Federation of Labor denounced Johnson for his "anti-labor" voting record in Congress, and endorsed

Coke Stevenson. Johnson countered by taking the "Johnson City Windmill" all over Texas, defending his record. and denouncing Stevenson.

July 14-16   Harry S Truman and Alben W. Barkley nominated for President and Vice-President by the Democratic National Convention.

July 24   Stevenson defeated Johnson in the Primary 477,077 votes to 405,617. However, since none of the candidates received a clear-cut majority, a run-off primary was set for August.

July 25   Flew to Washington for talks with Congressional and Administration officials on foreign and military affairs. Johnson took this action to impress many Texas voters as a man familiar with big problems, and to counteract Stevenson who was doing the exact same thing.

August 26   Made an airplane tour of Texas cities culminating in a huge rally in Dallas. Lady Bird accompanied him on most of his tours during this campaign, even speaking, herself, at several rallies and meetings.

August 28   Early election returns indicated that Stevenson led Johnson by 1,894 votes.

September 2   Texas Election Bureau announced that vote was complete, and that Stevenson had won the primary by 362 votes. The Bureau, however, reminded the public that its own count was unofficial.

September 4   Precinct 13 in the county seat of Alice in Jim Wells County revised its vote. Instead of the originally reported 765 total for Johnson and 60 for Stevenson, its new figures read 967 for Johnson and 61 for Stevenson. Johnson now led by 87 votes and had won the election. Political boss George Parr had been instrumental in "finding" the additional Johnson votes, and Coke Stevenson knew it.

September 15   At the State Democratic Executive Committee meeting, Johnson was officially declared the winner of the Senate primary election. Alvin Wirtz had been instrumental in securing the victory for Johnson.

Texas State Democratic Convention certified Johnson's

nomination, but Stevenson secured a temporary injunction from Federal District Court Judge T. Whitfield Davidson of Dallas barring Johnson's name from the November ballot until a hearing in Federal Court in Fort Worth could be held on September 21.

September 21 Hearing held in Fort Worth. Judge Davidson upheld his restraining order until United States commissioners could investigate the voting in Jim Wells and Duval Counties.

September 28 Justice Hugo Black of the Supreme Court, and presiding Judge of the Fifth Circuit, which covered six states, including Texas, issued an order setting aside Judge Davidson's ruling that barred Johnson's name from appearing on the November ballot. Black ruled that Federal courts lacked jurisdiction over state elections, and on this basis, the case had to revert to the state court that ruled Johnson must be dismissed. The negotiations with Black in behalf of Johnson were conducted by a Memphis, Tennessee lawyer named Abe Fortas.

October 6 The United States Supreme Court upheld Justice Black's ruling allowing Johnson's name to appear on the ballot.

November 3 Defeated Republican opponent Congressman John Porter by 350,000 votes for the Senate seat from Texas. Truman carried the state by a half a million votes over Thomas E. Dewey.

1949

January 3 Sworn into his seat in the Senate along with eighteen other freshmen Senators. Johnson was appointed to the powerful Armed Services Committee of the Senate, and to the Interstate and Foreign Commerce Committee which exerted a strong influence on the Federal Communications Commission.

March 9 Delivered his maiden speech to the Senate voicing his opposition to extend Senate Rule XXII (Cloture Rule) to motions as well as actual bills. Called President Truman a dictator. The Senate voted down the motion to extend the Cloture Rule, and when it did, Truman's Fair Deal was dead.

March 15 Co-sponsored a rule change that would require the affirmative vote of two-thirds of the Senate's entire membership to put Cloture into effect. This further extension of power for the Southern bloc in the Senate was approved as the new Rule XXII. As a result of his actions in the Cloture fight, Johnson became the new protege of Senator Richard Russell of Georgia.

September 27 Served as Chairman of the Commerce Committee's Sub-Committee conducting hearings on Truman's reappointment of Leland Olds as Chairman of the Federal Power Commission. Johnson, Senator Robert Kerr of Oklahoma, and others opposed the FPC's regulation of natural gas prices. Johnson and Kerr's strategy was to smear Olds so as to bring about the Senate's rejection of his nomination, and indirectly discredit the FPC's regulation of natural gas prices.

October 5 Voted in favor of Truman's arms aid program. This was a rare occasion since Johnson repeatedly voted against the Truman Administration's proposals on such things as civil rights, off shore oil rights, and minimum wage legislation. In addition, he supported Senator Pat McCarran's anti-Eastern and anti-Southern European peoples Immigration Bill and voted to override Truman's veto of it.

October 12 Had done his work well in the Olds hearing as the Senate rejected Old's reappointment by a vote of 53 to 15. However, the Senate failed to limit the FPC's jurisdiction over natural gas prices.

1950

February 9 Senator Joseph McCarthy of Wisconsin began his "witch hunt" of alleged Communists in the Federal government in a speech at Wheeling, West Virginia.

June 25 Communist North Korean troops crossed the thirty-eighth parallel and invaded South Korea.

June 26 Defended Truman's actions in Korea in a speech to the Senate.

July 17 Named Chairman of the Senate Preparedness Investigating Subcommittee of the Senate Armed Services Committee, despite his lack of seniority. Named Senators Estes Kefauver, Virgil Chapman, and Lester Hunt to sit on the Subcommittee. Republican Senators Styles Bridges, Leverett

Saltonstall and Wayne Morse were also named by the Armed Services Committee.

July 31   First meeting of the Preparedness Subcommittee took place. Johnson was highly critical of Truman for not mobilizing the nation and installing World War II controls to fight the North Koreans. He was particularly critical of Secretary of Defense Louis Johnson whom Truman shortly removed. Truman and the press commended the Johnson Committee.

October 2   Truman ordered General MacArthur to cross the thirty-eighth parallel into North Korea, but to stop at the Manchurian border.

November 26   Communist Chinese armies crossed into North Korea, and engaged American troops in battle. Hysteria flamed across the United States.

1951

January 2   Elected by acclamation as Majority Whip of the Senate at the Democratic Caucus. Johnson was now the number two man in the Senate's hierarchy after only two years as a member. Senator Ernest McFarland of Arizona was chosen as Majority leader after a tough fight between liberal and conservative Senate Democrats. Johnson continued as Chairman of the Preparedness Subcommittee despite his duties as Majority Whip.

April 11   MacArthur was relieved of command in Korea by President Truman. As a member of the Armed Services Committee, Johnson participated in the Senate's MacArthur hearings, sometimes serving as alternate Chairman with Senator Richard Russell.

October 27   Johnson's "Texas Daddy" Alvin Wirtz died of a heart attack. Johnson flew to Texas to attend the funeral. He was now forced to handle his own state political relations, with Wirtz gone, and he faced a tough fight with the then Governor of Texas, Allan Shivers, who had become the State's top politician, and who might present a menace to the national party in 1952 by taking Texas into the Republican camp. Johnson also feared that Shivers might try to unseat him in the Senate in 1954.

1952

January 3	Elected as Majority Whip of the Senate at the Democratic Caucus for a second time.
May 27	With Governor Shivers completely in control of the Texas State Convention neither Johnson nor Rayburn bothered to attend. Shivers succeeded in having a non-committed delegation to the National Convention chosen.
July 7-11	The Republican National Convention selected Dwight D. Eisenhower and Richard M. Nixon as their candidates.
July 21	Johnson decided to join with Shivers so as to protect his Senate seat in 1954. As a result, he succeeded in getting the handpicked Shivers delegation seated at the National Convention in Chicago much to the chagrin of the loyalist Texas delegation headed by an old time friend of Johnson's, Maury Maverick. Shivers did not firmly pledge to support the national ticket.
July 23-26	Attended Democratic National Convention in Chicago, and was placed in the uncomfortable position of being a Senator Richard Russell supporter at the same time that Sam Rayburn's nomination for President was being considered.
July 25	Adlai Stevenson was selected as the Democratic Party's Presidential candidate on the third ballot after President Truman flew to Chicago and scolded the delegates for their failure to select his choice, Stevenson. Senator John Sparkman of Alabama was Stevenson's running mate. Johnson was luke-warm to Stevenson's candidacy.
September 9	At the Governor's Convention in Amarillo, Texas, Shivers denounced the Stevenson-Sparkman ticket, and urged all Democrats to vote for Eisenhower. Nevertheless, Johnson continued to appease Shivers.
October 17	Introduced Stevenson at Forth Worth. Johnson was unenthusiastic and the Fort Worth rally proved the coldest of the Stevenson Campaign tours of Texas.
November 4	Eisenhower and Nixon defeated Stevenson and Sparkman 442 electoral votes to 89. Eisenhower had 33.9 million popular votes, Stevenson 27.3 million. Stevenson lost Texas

by more than a million votes, and was convinced that Johnson should be numbered among those who contributed to his defeat in the Lone Star state. The Republicans captured both Houses by slim majorities as well.

1953

January 3 With Senator Richard Russell's help, Johnson was elected Senate Minority Leader, Democratic Party Conference Chairman, and Democratic Policy Committee Chairman at the Democratic Caucus. The Caucus accepted Johnson's choice of Earle Clements of Kentucky as Minority Whip.

January 13 After the Senate Republican Caucus removed Wayne Morse of Oregon from his committee assignments because he had supported Stevenson in 1952, Johnson refused to let him stay on his committees as part of the Democratic Party's quota of members. Morse was furious with Johnson and vowed that he would campaign against him in Texas in 1954.

May 5 Voted in favor of the Tidelands Oil Bill which gave offshore oil rights to Texas, Louisiana and California.

July 26 A truce ending the Korean War was signed at Panmunjan.

July 31 Senate Majority Leader Robert Taft died. "Mr. Republican's" death made Johnson the number one man in the Senate despite his being only the Minority Leader. President Eisenhower came to depend on him more and more to aid passage of his legislative program.

October 1 Johnson began his 1954 campaign in the fall of 1953, starting with an extensive "nonpolitical" tour of Texas.

1954

February 26 Voted for the so-called Bricker Amendment to limit the power of the President in making Executive Agreements. The vote was 60 to 31, just one short of the necessary two-thirds majority. Johnson had been one of the 62 Senators who had joined Senator John W. Bricker of Ohio in sponsoring the bill, and the final debate and vote was on a version as amended by Senator Walter F. George of Georgia.

March 10 Met with Eisenhower and other Congressional leaders to discuss the worsening situation in Indochina. The President announced that he had sent 200 air force technicians to Indochina to accompany a large number of B26's that he had also sent to Indochina for French use. Johnson stated that he was opposed to the sending of the 200 Americans to Indochina.

March 20   France asked for United States military intervention in Indochina.

April 3   Johnson and a group of Congressional leaders met with Secretary of State John Foster Dulles who asked them to support the use of American air forces in Indochina. The Senators and Congressmen refused, but Johnson and Russell offered their own three point program—U.S. intervention in Indochina must be a coalition with the British Commonwealth and the neighboring countries to Indochina; the U.S. must not be made to appear to be fighting to save French colonialism; and the French must remain in the war and not pull out. He called Eisenhower's policy weak.

April 26   The Geneva Conference began to determine the fate of Indochina with the United States, France, Great Britain, the Soviet Union, Communist China, South Vietnam, North Vietnam, Laos, and Cambodia represented.

May 8   The French surrendered to the North Vietnamese at Dienbienphu. This defeat marked the end of effective French military strength in Southeast Asia.

June 17   The Army-McCarthy hearings ended with such damage to Senator McCarthy that Republican Senators stated that he should be punished.

June 26   Issued the "Johnson Doctrine" which proposed treating Communist and Communist oriented regimes differently from other dictatorships. His resolution limited action solely to Communist penetration of the Western Hemisphere, and was prompted by the Communist takeover in Guatamala, and the subsequent CIA inspired invasion of Guatamala from Honduras through the person of the rightist, Colonel Carlos Castillo Armas.

July 21   Declaration of the Geneva Conference was not signed by the United States or South Vietnam. The Declaration divided Vietnam at the 17th parallel (North and South Vietnam created). Unification would depend upon elections scheduled for 1956 which were never held, and the French withdrew their troops.

July 24   In a tough and dirty primary campaign and election, Johnson defeated Dudley Dougherty, 875,000 to 350,000 votes. On the same night, Johnson joined with Senator Knowland to break up the Liberal Democratic filibuster against revision of the Atomic Energy Act of 1946 which they charged was a nuclear giveaway to big business.

July 30   Republican Senator Ralph Flanders of Vermont offered a resolution to censure Senator Joseph McCarthy for bringing the Senate into disrepute.

August 2   Offered Joint-Proposal with Majority Leader Knowland of California to set up a six man committee to study the charges of misconduct against Senator McCarthy. Johnson appointed three Democratic Conservatives to the committee—John Stennis of Mississippi, Sam Ervin of North Carolina, and Edward Johnson of Colorado.

August 11   Johnson's opening move toward becoming Majority Leader came when his Lieutenant, Hubert Humphrey, introduced a bill to outlaw the Communist Party. Republicans were intending to concentrate on the "soft on Communism" line to beat Humphrey in Minnesota, and Johnson worked out this legislative ploy to kill the Republican campaign before it began. Johnson also pushed the Communist Control Bill of 1954 through the Senate which passed it by a vote of 80 to 0.

September 27 The Senate Committee on the McCarthy Censure issued its report. It called for censure on two counts: McCarthy's contempt for the Senate, and his vicious treatment of General Ralph Zwicker.

October 24   The United States promised aid to South Vietnam.

November 2   Reelected to the Senate quite easily. Democrats regained control of the Congress with a 29 seat majority in the

House, and a 1 seat margin in the Senate. Wayne Morse, Johnson's old enemy, was again the pivotal vote, but Johnson won him to the Democratic side by promising him a seat on the Senate Foreign Relations Committee. Morse's vote made Johnson the Majority Leader.

December 2   McCarthy censured in the Senate by a vote of 67 to 22. Johnson supported the censure resolution as did all the Democratic Senators except John Fitzgerald Kennedy of Massachusetts who was then in a hospital. Johnson took full credit for Democratic solidarity on the vote.

December 2-4 Suffered severe back pains which kept him from attending the Democratic National Committee Meeting in New Orleans. Without Johnson there to maneuver, the Committee chose Paul Butler of Indiana, Adlai Stevenson's choice, as the National Committee Chairman. Stevenson again presented a roadblock to Johnson's Presidential ambitions.

1955

January 5   Elected Senate Majority Leader, Democratic Policy Committee Chairman, and Democratic Conference Chairman. Senate Liberals were unwilling to accept him unquestioningly as their spokesman.

January 9   Went to the Mayo Clinic in Rochester, Minnesota, for a medical examination. Johnson's back pains had become more severe, and he was suffering from a kidney stone. Johnson was absent from the Senate for two months.

March 8   Returned to the Senate to assume his duties as Majority Leader despite warning of the Mayo Clinic internist, Dr. James C. Cain who told him he might suffer a relapse if he did not rest.

June 7   Helped to defeat the Capehart Amendment to the Public Housing Bill. The Bill was sponsored by Senator Sparkman and proposed the construction of 100,000 housing units a year. The Capehart Amendment, proposed by Senator Homer Capehart of Iowa, would have permitted the small number of 35,000 housing units to be started each year. Johnson temporarily gained the support of the Liberals for this piece of work.

July 2   Suffered severe heart attack at George Brown's estate, *Huntlands,* in Virginia. Was immediately taken to Bethesda Naval Hospital. Was released from the hospital on August 7.

July 18-23   Geneva Summit Meeting took place. Eisenhower and Premier Nikolai Bulganin of the Soviet Union failed to agree on the unification of Germany.

August 25   Flew to the L.B.J. Ranch in Texas to complete his recuperation. While at the ranch for a five month convalescence, Johnson was visited by many important personages including Rayburn, Kefauver, Bridges, and Stevenson. Despite his weak condition, Johnson began making forays back into politics. Returned to Washington in December.

November 15   Stevenson announced his candidacy for the 1956 nomination. Johnson, too, began promoting himself for the nomination in November.

December 29   Had checkup at the Mayo Clinic where six physicians attested to his complete recovery.

December 30   Announced that he would continue his duties as Senate Majority Leader.

1956

January 3   Applauded by his colleagues when the second session of the Eighty-Fourth Congress convened.

February 6   Pushed the Harris-Fulbright Bill through the Senate by a vote of 53 to 38. The Bill, sponsored by Senator J. William Fulbright and Representative Merton Harris, removed Federal control over natural gas prices. President Eisenhower vetoed it a month later.

March 11   Did not sign the Declaration of Constitutional Principles which was issued by one hundred Southern Senators and Congressmen. The "Southern Manifesto" pledged to use "all lawful means" to reverse the Supreme Court's 1954 edict barring segregation in the public schools. Johnson refrained from signing it because he felt it might have endangered his position as Majority Leader. However, he told reporters that he was not a civil rights advocate.

April 10   Announced his availability to serve as Chairman of the

Texas delegation to the National Democratic Convention. Governor Shivers made the same announcement, and Johnson decided to end his years of appeasing Shivers and to fight him for control of the Texas Democratic Party.

April 14   "Lyndon Johnson for President" Committee was formed in Austin by E.H. Perry and Thomas Miller, two of Johnson's old Texas friends.

May 22   Texas State Convention gave Johnson a landslide victory over Shivers in their battle for party control. Johnson was named Chairman of the Texas delegation to the National Convention, and its "favorite son" candidate for the Presidential nomination.

July 23-   Killed all chances of Senate passage of the Administration's
August 10   Civil Rights Bill by parliamentary maneuvering. He referred the Bill to Mississippi Senator James Eastland's Judiciary Committee, where it died. Because of his actions, Johnson alienated the Civil Rights Liberals.

August 13-17 Attended the National Democratic Convention in Chicago as Chairman of the Texas delegation. Refused to support Stevenson at the Convention, wanting the nomination himself.

August 16   Johnson was nominated for President by John Connally, while the seconding speech was made by Allen Frear of Delaware.

Stevenson was nominated on the first ballot. Johnson received 80 votes. Kefauver was selected as the Vice-Presidential candidate on the second ballot defeating John F. Kennedy by a narrow margin. Kennedy had called on Johnson asking for his support. Johnson gave the Texas vote to Kennedy on the second ballot, but his attempt at being a kingmaker failed when the Convention nominated Kefauver. Johnson and Rayburn did succeed in getting a mild civil rights plank into the platform.

August 20   The Republican National Convention meeting in San Francisco renominated Eisenhower and Nixon.

September 11 Attended Texas State Governor's Convention in Fort Worth as head of his county delegation. Johnson completely dominated the Convention, succeeded in getting Price Daniel nominated for Governor, and pushed through his own platform with ease.

October 21   A revolt in Poland led to the establishment of a nationalist Communist government.

October 23   A revolt in Hungary was begun by students, writers, and politicians against Russian rule. It was crushed by the Soviets on November 4.

October 29   Suez crisis began as Israel invaded Egypt, followed by Britain and France on October 31. The crisis was ended on November 6 when the Soviets threatened to aid Egypt, and the United States refused to back Great Britain. A cease-fire was established.

November 6   Eisenhower and Nixon scored a landside victory over Stevenson and Kefauver. The electoral vote was 457 to 74, and the popular vote was 35,600,000 for Eisenhower, 26,000,000 for Stevenson. Both Houses of Congress, however, remained in Democratic hands. Again, Johnson did not actively campaign for Stevenson, and with his defeat, the road was now clear for Johnson to build for the 1960 Presidential race.

1957

January 3   Reelected Majority Leader of the Senate in a close race. Senator Mike Mansfield of Montana was chosen as Majority Whip.

January 6   Gave a seat on the Senate Foreign Relations Committee to Senator John F. Kennedy in order to prevent Kefauver, a 1960 Presidential aspirant, from gaining recognition as a Democratic Party foreign policy spokesman. Johnson did not regard Kennedy's candidacy for 1960 with much alarm.

February 20   Met with President Eisenhower and fifteen other Congressional leaders in the White House to discuss the proposed U.N. sanctions against Israel. Refused to agree to a public statement favoring sanctions against Israel. The question of sanctions never came to a head, for on March 1, Israel withdrew from occupied Eygptian territory.

March 5   The Senate passed the Johnson version of the Eisenhower Doctrine by a vote of 72 to 19. The Doctrine empowered the President to use armed force to defend the independence of a Middle-Eastern country. Johnson had eliminated a separate Middle-Eastern fund, and assigned such aid under the regular foreign aid appropriations. He also deleted Congressional authorization for military aid and left this entirely to the President. Eisenhower signed it into law on March 9.

April 2   Attempted to prevent Ralph Yarborough from being elected to the Senate in a special election in Texas. Johnson failed as Yarborough won the election by 75,000 votes. Johnson, thereupon, appointed the new Senator to two minor Senate committees.

May 15   In a Senate speech, Johnson demanded that the budget be cut. During the "battle of the budget," Johnson was given a free hand by Appropriations Chairman Carl Hayden of Arizona. When the last cut had been made, the 1957 Eisenhower budget had been reduced by 5.5 billion dollars. The President was furious, but could do nothing.

June 20   Attempted to send Administration's 1957 Civil Rights Bill to Senator Eastland's Judiciary Committee, but the Senate put the Bill directly on the Calendar by a vote of 45 to 39. Senator Kennedy voted with Johnson on this matter.

July 2-   A great Senate debate over the Administration's Civil Rights
August 28   Bill took place.

August 2   Johnson's Jury Trial Amendment to the Civil Rights Bill passed the Senate by a vote of 51 to 42. In essence, the Amendment made certain that anyone who deprived a Negro of his right to vote, and continued to do so after an injunction was issued by a Federal Judge, could not be tried for contempt solely by that Judge, but was entitled to a jury trial by his Southern neighbors.

August 28   Engineered the passage of the watered-down Civil Rights Bill of 1957 through the Senate. This measure created a six man Civil Rights Commission, while District Courts were authorized to issue injunctions to protect civil rights, and voting cases would be heard without benefit of juries.

September 9   President Eisenhower signed the almost useless Civil Rights Act. Johnson gained a reputation as a champion of civil rights legislation in 1957, although his compromise tactics in guiding the Bill through the Senate allowed him to continue his good relations with the Southern Senate bloc.

October 4   The Soviet Union gained great prestige by sending an earth satellite, *Sputnik I,* into an outer space orbit. This Soviet first caused marked concern in the United States. Johnson now began to push for a speeded-up space program.

1958

January 7   At the Democratic Senate Caucus, Johnson delivered his own "State of the Union Message." He called for strengthened national defenses, and a United States policy aimed at winning control of outer space.

January 31   The United States successfully launched an earth satellite, *Explorer I.*

February 1   Syria and Egypt merged as the United Arab Republic, and became the center of pro-Soviet influence in the Mid-East.

February 8   Assumed the role of Democratic leader of the Space Age, when he introduced a resolution to establish a Senate Committee on Aeronautical and Space Sciences. The Senate approved by a vote of 78 to 1, and Johnson became Chairman of the new committee.

March 27   Nikita S. Khrushchev became Premier of the Soviet Union.

May 9   Syria supported a revolt in Lebanon against pro-U.S. President Camille Chamoun.

July 15   President Eisenhower sent American Marines into Lebanon at the request of President Chamoun. Johnson strongly approved of the President's action in a speech before the Senate.

August 23   The Chinese Communists renewed the shelling of Quemoy and Matsu, prompting the United States to give emergency aid to Chiang Kai-shek. Johnson steered the appropriation through the Senate easily.

September 12   Johnson's mother died in Texas. He flew to Johnson City for the funeral.

October 25   United States troops left Lebanon, which gradually resumed a neutral position.

November 4   The Democrats won smashing victories in the elections. They gained 15 seats in the Senate and 48 in the House. The most noticeable victory was the reelection of Senator John F. Kennedy in Massachusetts (860,000 vote majority). Kennedy was clearly stepping up his drive for the Presidential nomination in 1960.

November 10   Selected by President Eisenhower to represent the United States at the United Nations debate on outer space control. Johnson called for peaceful cooperation in his speech before the U.N. delegates on November 17.

Berlin Crisis began when Premier Khrushchev announced that the Soviet Union was about to turn over its Berlin Zone to East Germany, and demanded that the Western powers do likewise. If they refused, he said, they would have to deal with the East German government on all Berlin matters.

November 27   Khrushchev threatened to sign a peace treaty with East Germany if the West did not get out of Berlin within six months.

1959

January 7   Reelected Majority Leader of the Senate. At the Democratic Caucus, he delivered his "State of the Union Address" in which he strongly criticized the Eisenhower Administration. Also announced that there would be no further Democratic caucuses in 1959.

January 8   Charles DeGaulle became first President of the Fifth French Republic.

January 9   Engineered the defeat of a motion by the Liberal Democrats for a simple majority vote to invoke cloture. The vote in the Senate was 60 to 36.

January 12   Pushed through a motion to return the Cloture Rule to its pre-1949 status, so a filibuster could be ended by the vote of two-thirds of the Senators present rather than the existing requirements of two-thirds of the entire Senate membership.

February 16 After leading a two year revolution in Cuba, Fidel Castro became Premier of Cuba after President Fulgencio Batista resigned. Castro announced his alliance with Communism and the Soviet Union.

April 22 The Senate passed the McClellan Amendment, sponsored by Senator John McClellan of Arkansas; this Amendment was added to the Kennedy sponsored Labor Anti-racketeering Bill which proposed to reform internal union operations so as to prevent racketeers from gaining control of a union. The McClellan Amendment permitted a union member to go to Federal Court over any point of disagreement he had with union leaders. This could conceivably disrupt every labor organization in the country to the point of chaos. Kennedy asked Johnson to allow him to floor-manage the Bill, an area Johnson invariably reserved for himself. But, Kennedy's floor-managing skill was inefficient, and Johnson gave him no help. In the end, the Senate passed an extremely stringent anti-labor law, the Landrum-Griffin Bill, instead of the Kennedy legislation. Johnson had successfully embarrassed the Massachusetts Senator.

May 11-
August 5 Foreign Ministers' Conference met at Geneva, but no agreement was reached on Berlin. Khrushchev, anxious for a summit conference, allowed the deadline on Berlin to pass without any action.

September 15 Premier Khrushchev arrived in Washington for a tour of the United States. Johnson, not wishing to permit Khrushchev to address a Joint Session of Congress, adjourned the Senate six hours before Khrushchev's expected arrival. In order to do this, Johnson had the Senate pass 166 bills between September 12 and the 6:22 A.M. adjournment of the Senate on September 15. Johnson was also anxious to end this session of Congress so that he could go home to campaign for the Presidency.

October 17 Sam Rayburn opened a twelve room "Johnson for President" headquarters in Austin, Texas.

October 20 Began Presidential campaign tour through Texas after having told Robert F. Kennedy, who had come to the L.B.J.

Ranch that he had no intention of running for President.

1960

January 2　　John F. Kennedy formally announced his candidacy for the Democratic Presidential nomination.

January 6　　At the Democratic Senate Caucus, Johnson announced that he would convene a caucus anytime any Senator requested one.

January 13　Convened another session of the Democratic Caucus. The Democratic Senators voted 51 to 12 to allow Johnson to continue as total boss of the Democratic Policy Committee, although Democratic Liberals were attacking him at this time.

January 18　Convened another caucus to discuss specific tax legislation for the session as the Liberals badgered him to take this action. At the end of the meeting, he announced that he would not call another caucus during the rest of the session even though it might cost him delegation support at the National Convention.

January 25　Announced that he would seek reelection to the Senate from Texas.

February 15　Began Senate action on additional civil rights legislation. Attacked by Senate Conservatives, especially Senator Russell of Georgia. Nevertheless, the battle over the Civil Rights Bill was begun. The Southern Senators filibustered, and the debate lasted fifty-three days. Johnson took this opportunity to visit Illinois and New York to push the Civil Rights Bill, and to talk to politicians concerning the Presidential nomination.

February 29　Undertook to break the Southern filibuster. Put the Senate into continuous, round-the-clock session. This Senate day lasted until March 8, when Johnson succeeded in pushing through the Senate a compromise Civil Rights Bill which extended the life of the Civil Rights Commission, established a Federal referee device to enlarge Negro registration in the South, (only for Federal elections) and made it a Federal crime for anyone to make bomb threats by mail, telephone or telegraph.

April 5
Kennedy won the Wisconsin Presidential Primary. Johnson still did not declare himself, stating that he had no time to campaign, and that somebody had "to mind the store" in the Capital.

April 23
On the advice of Rayburn, Johnson went to Colorado, Wyoming, Utah, and Nevada for talks with Democratic politicians concerning the National Convention.

May 1-16
A United States U-2 photo reconnaissance plane was shot down 1,300 miles within Soviet Territory. Khrushchev announced on May 7 that the pilot, Francis Gary Powers, was alive, and had confessed to spying. On May 11, President Eisenhower took full responsibility for the U-2 flights, and on May 16, Khrushchev used the U-2 incident as an excuse for refusing to attend the summit talks in Paris.

May 6
President Eisenhower signed the Civil Rights Bill into law. The press praised Johnson for his efforts in this legislative action.

May 7
Won renomination to the Senate in the Texas Senatorial Primary.

May 10
Kennedy won the West Virginia Primary, and gained tremendous prestige in his race for the Presidential nomination. Johnson still did not declare himself.

July 5
Finally declared himself an official candidate for the Democratic Presidential nomination. He had run an ineffective campaign, had not entered any primaries, and had made only a few, limited campaign trips to garner delegates.

July 12
Participated in a televised debate with Kennedy before the Massachusetts and Texas delegations at the Democratic National Convention in Los Angeles.

July 13
Nominated for the Presidency by Sam Rayburn, but was defeated on the first ballot by Kennedy who received 806 votes to Johnson's 409. He had started too late with too little.

July 14
Kennedy asked him if he wanted the Vice-Presidential nomination. After several hours of confusion, conferences, and political deals, Johnson accepted the offer. Thereupon, Kennedy announced Johnson as his choice for Vice-President.

Johnson was nominated for Vice-President by Governor David Lawrence of Pennsylvania, and the Convention approved by acclamation on the first ballot. Johnson's selection, it was hoped, would bring unity to the Democratic Party in the election. Johnson accepted the nomination the next day.

July 25 The Republican Party meeting in Chicago nominated Richard M. Nixon for President, and Henry Cabot Lodge of Massachusetts for Vice-President.

August 6 A Texas court ruled that it was legal for Johnson's name to appear on the Texas ballot for both the office of Vice-President and Senator.

August 8 The Senate reconvened. It was an awkward situation since Johnson was the top Senator, but Kennedy was now the top Democrat. Kennedy decided to manage some of the Senate Bills personally. All of those he managed failed to pass by the time Congress adjourned. Kennedy could campaign well, but Johnson still ran the Senate.

September 12 Campaigned with Kennedy in Texas. Kennedy counted on Johnson to bring in the 24 Texas electoral votes in November. During the campaign, Johnson went to 43 states but like other Vice-Presidential candidates in the past, he garnered insignificant newspaper coverage.

October 6-23 Made a 3,500 mile campaign tour through the South in a private train called the *L.B.J. Victory Special.*

October 18 Khrushchev announced that he would await the election of a new American President before settling Berlin crisis.

November 5 Closed out campaign with Kennedy in a giant "recapitulation rally" at New York's Madison Square Garden.

November 8 Kennedy and Johnson defeated Nixon and Lodge. Kennedy received 34.2 million votes (303 electoral) to Nixon's 34.1 million votes (219 electoral). Congress remained Democratic and Johnson was reelected to the Senate. Texas went for Kennedy and Johnson and the 24 Texas electoral votes went into the Democratic column.

1961

January 3   The First Democratic Caucus met. Johnson was still a Senator and Majority Leader. He asked to be allowed to attend future democratic caucuses, and his request was granted by a vote of 46 to 17. Mike Mansfield was chosen Majority Leader, and Hubert Humphrey was selected Majority Whip. In the afternoon, Johnson was sworn in for his third term as Senator from Texas, and, of course, resigned that office three minutes later. William Blakely, was then sworn in as appointed Senator.

VICE-PRESIDENT

January 20   Inaugurated Vice President of the United States. The oath of office was administered by Speaker Rayburn in the first such action ever performed by a Speaker of the House.

January 21   Presided over the Senate for the first time. Johnson was uncomfortable in his new post, as he found himself on the outside looking into a situation he had once completely controlled.

February 20   Colonel John Glenn became the first American to orbit the earth in a space vehicle. In late January, President Kennedy had appointed Johnson, Chairman of the Space Council, but the Vice-President's Committee was nothing more than a paper organization with very little power.

March 6   Kennedy established the President's Committee on Equal Employment Opportunity for firms with government contracts. Johnson was appointed Chairman of the Committee, and drafted, with Abe Fortas, a tough Executive Order, for Kennedy's signature, that forced all private contractors on government projects to sign statements that they didn't practice discrimination. The Committee would then possess authority to cancel contracts of violators. Kennedy signed the order. Within the first ten months, the Committee performed admirable work in ending discrimination in firms doing business with the government.

April 9-15   Made official fact-finding and good will trip to Africa and Europe at the request of President Kennedy. Johnson delivered the main address at the Tenth Anniversary celebration of SHAPE in Paris. During his Vice-Presidency, Johnson made a number of official trips totaling 120,000 miles that took him to 33 different countries throughout the world.

April 15-17   Invasion of Cuba by 1,400 Cuban refugees was crushed at the Bay of Pigs by Castro's forces. The CIA trained and equipped the invaders, who failed partly from lack of promised air support. Kennedy told Johnson nothing of this venture. Johnson told Kennedy that the CIA officials responsible for this blunder should be fired.

May 5-19   Made fact-finding and good will tour of Southeast Asia and the Far East. Gave his report to Kennedy on May 24, calling the trip an unqualified success.

June 3-4   Kennedy and Khrushchev met in Vienna to discuss the question of Germany. Khrushchev threatened to sign a treaty with East Germany and to declare West Berlin a "free city." The Vienna Summit Conference accomplished nothing.

July 13   At a meeting of the National Security Council on the situation in Germany, Johnson advised Kennedy to avoid any further diplomatic negotiations with the Soviets, and to concentrate on a military showdown. He called for a state of national emergency, an increase of five billion dollars in the defense budget, a call-up of the reserves, a 2 per-cent tax increase, and a standby order for wage and price controls. Kennedy favored the Johnson approach but in a milder form.

August 13   The agreements for free access within Berlin were broken by Khrushchev, as the Soviets began erecting a wall between East and West Berlin.

August 19-22 Sent to Germany by President Kennedy to assure the West Berliners of United States support in the Berlin crisis. His trip was a great success, as he was very warmly received by the Germans.

1962

April 10   Hailed by President Kennedy and Congressional leaders on the occasion of his twenty-fifth year of Federal government service.

May 15	Kennedy sent 4,000 troops to Thailand in order to strengthen the anti-Communist position in Laos.
June 11	Geneva Conference on Laos set up a neutralist government under Souvanna Phouma.
August 23	Left the United States for a good will tour of the Mediterranean area countries.
September 8	Had an audience with Pope John XXIII at the Vatican in Rome. Returned to Washington on September 22.
October 14	Cuban Missile Crisis began as the United States discovered that the Soviets were installing missile sites on Cuba with a range covering most of the United States.
October 20	Chinese Communists invaded India at Ladakh and in Assam Province. In response, the United States sent military aid to India.
October 22	President Kennedy ordered the Soviet Union to withdraw its missiles and imposed a quarantine by naval blockade on Cuba. The United States and the Soviet Union reached agreement over the Cuban missiles on October 28 when Khrushchev removed the missiles and Kennedy promised not to invade Cuba. Johnson was not consulted much during the crisis, but he did state that the answer should be an all-out military liberation of Cuba. Kennedy considered Johnson's views too extreme to follow.
November 21	Chinese Communists withdrew from India.
	Kennedy lifted the blockade on Cuba after the Soviets gave assurances that the missiles had been removed.

1963

February 28	Represented the United States at the inaguration of President Juan Bosch of the Dominican Republic.
April 3	Martin Luther King began to lead mass demonstrations in Birmingham, Alabama, to desegregate the city.
June 17	Attended the funeral of Pope John XXIII in Rome as the official representative of the United States.

August 5   A Nuclear Test Ban Treaty was signed by which the United States, Soviet Union, and Great Britain agreed not to test nuclear weapons in the atmosphere. France did not sign although she had exploded her first nuclear bomb in February, 1960.

August 28   Martin Luther King gave his "I have a dream" speech before a massive throng at the Lincoln Memorial in Washington following a great civil rights march on the nation's capital.

September 3-17   Made a two week good will tour of the Benelux and Scandinavian countries. Reported to President Kennedy upon his return to the United States.

October 5   Governor John Connally of Texas visited the White House to arrange a trip to Texas for President Kennedy. The trip was scheduled for November 21-22, and Johnson was to accompany the President who was trying to mend some political splits in the Lone Star State.

October 8   Bobby Baker, the Secretary of the Senate, and a longtime Johnson protege, resigned his Senate post. Baker was under suspicion of being involved in a number of shady deals and scandals prompting the Senate to call for a special investigation of the whole matter.

November 1 A military coup in South Vietnam overthrew the corrupt and inefficient regime of South Vietnamese President Ngo Dinh Diem, who was later executed.

November 22 Johnson was in the second car of the motorcade taking President Kennedy through Dallas, Texas. The President was assassinated and Governor Connally seriously wounded. Lee Harvey Oswald, the suspected killer, was quickly caught, but was himself murdered by a Dallas night club owner, Jack Ruby, in the Dallas jail in front of nationwide television audiences.

FIRST TERM

November 22 Sworn in as the thirty-sixth President of the United States by Judge Sarah T. Hughes of the Northern District of Texas aboard *Air Force One* at Love Field, Dallas. Johnson had made the decision to be sworn in on the plane before taking off for Washington. He also decided that Kennedy's remains would travel to Washington with him aboard *Air Force One.* In Washington, the Treasury Department noted a change in Administration by increasing Johnson's salary from $35,000 to $100,000 a year starting at 2:00 P.M. that day. Johnson landed in Washington at 5:05 P.M.

All the cabinet members from the Kennedy Administration continued in office. They included: Dean Rusk, Secretary of State, C. Douglas Dillon, Secretary of the Treasury, Robert McNamara, Secretary of Defense, Robert F. Kennedy, Attorney General, John A. Gronouski, Postmaster General, Stewart Udall, Secretary of the Interior, Orville Freeman, Secretary of Agriculture, Luther Hodges, Secretary of Commerce, W. Willard Wirtz, Secretary of Labor, and Anthony Celebrezze, Secretary of Health, Education and Welfare.

November 23 Issued Proclamation 3561 which announced a National Day of Mourning for President Kennedy. Attended the Kennedy funeral in Arlington on November 25.

November 27 Addressed Joint Session of Congress in what may be termed his "First Inaugural Address." Pledged he would continue Kennedy's program with the phrase "Let Us Continue." The Johnson objective in the immediate period following the assassination was to give the impression he had taken such complete charge of the Federal government that there would be no skip in the national heartbeat.

November 30 Appointed Special Commission to investigate the assassination of President Kennedy. Named Chief Justice Earl Warren as Chairman. The Committee, thereafter, was known as the "Warren Commission."

December 14 Stated that he firmly opposed proposed reductions in Foreign Aid funds.

December 16 Signed the Higher Education Facilities Act.

Signed Foreign Assistance Act for economic and military aid to free world nations.

December 17 Addressed United Nations General Assembly in New York and pledged United States cooperation with that international body.

December 20   Signed the ratification of the Chamizal Convention with Mexico settling long standing boundary dispute along the Texas border.

December 26   Appointed a committee to review foreign aid programs with Under-Secretary of State George W. Ball as chairman.

December 28-29   Met with West German Chancellor Ludwig Erhard at the L.B.J. Ranch in Texas for far ranging talks on foreign affairs.

1964

January 3   Established the President's Committee on Consumer Interests and appointed Mrs. Esther Peterson as its Chairman.

January 3   Delivered his first State of the Union message to Congress. He called for a "War on Poverty."

January 9-10   Mobs clashed with American troops in the Canal Zone over the issue of flying American and Panamanian flags.

January 14-15   Met with President Antonio Segni of Italy for talks concerned with continued cooperation by both nations. Secretary of State Dean Rusk and Foreign Minister Guiseppe Saragat were also present.

January 15   Accepted resignation of Theodore C. Sorensen as Special Counsel to the President. Shortly thereafter, one by one, the Kennedy aides either resigned or were removed by Johnson, who began replacing them with his own advisors.

January 21   Accepted resignation of Edward R. Murrow as Director of the United States Information Agency.

January 21-22   Met with Prime Minister Lester Pearson of Canada for discussions which resulted in the Columbia River Agreement and the Roosevelt Campobello Park Agreement. Both were conservation accords.

January 23   Announced adoption of the 24th Amendment to the Constitution of the United States which outlawed poll taxes in Federal elections.

January 29   Announced successful launching of the first satellite by Saturn I.

February 7   Declared United States' determination to guarantee the security of the Naval Base at Guantanamo, Cuba.

February 12   Appointed Sargent Shriver to direct the program to eliminate poverty. Shriver took office on October 16.

February 14   Bobby Baker appeared before the Senate Rules Committee who was investigating his operations while Secretary of the Senate. In two and a half hours, Baker took the Fifth Amendment 125 times.

February 17   The Supreme Court in Wesberry vs. Sanders ordered the states to realign their Congressional districts so that the districts would be substantially equal in population. This established in law the principle of "one man, one vote."

February 26   Signed Tax Bill providing for cuts of $11.5 billion and reducing withholding rate from 18 to 14 percent.

February 28   Appointed Carl T. Rowan as Director of the United States Information Agency.

March 6   Sent letter to Chairman Nikita Khrushchev about the situation in Cyprus.

March 16   Sent Special Message to Congress proposing a "Nationwide War on the Sources of Poverty."

April 3   Signed Joint Declaration with government of Panama to seek a peaceful solution to the problems confronting both nations.

April 9   Announced a moratorium in the Railroad Labor Dispute after a four hour meeting with Railway Union leaders. The dispute was settled on April 22.

April 15   Established the President's Committee on Manpower.

April 28   Urged Congress to pass Aid Bill for the Appalachian Region, one of the most depressed areas in the nation.

May 12   Signed Pesticide Control Bill.

May 18   Sent Special Message to Congress requesting additional funds for military operations in Vietnam.

May 27   Announced agreement between the United States and the Soviet Union for a Consular Convention.

May 28   Signed bill providing aid for Alaska which had recently suffered a disastrous earthquake.

June 1-2   Met with Prime Minister Levi Eshkol of Israel for talks concerning economic and military assistance.

June 20   Lieutenant General William C. Westmoreland was appointed commander of the United States forces in Vietnam by President Johnson.

June 29   Met with Ambassador Henry Cabot Lodge for talks on Vietnam. Lodge resigned that day. Lodge reappointed on August 12, 1965.

July 2   Appointed General Maxwell D. Taylor as new Ambassador to Vietnam.

Signed the Civil Rights Bill which was the most sweeping legislation of its kind in American history. The Bill strengthened Negro voting rights by Federal regulation of literacy tests. Other parts of the Act dealt with desegregation in public accommodations, and facilities, continuing school desegregation, increased powers for the Civil Rights Commission, and the establishment of an Equal Employment Opportunity Commission.

July 9   Signed the Urban Mass Transportation Act to provide Federal monies for the improvement and construction of roads and highways. In addition, funds were allocated for the planning and development of more efficient mass transit facilities.

July 13   The Republican Convention met in San Francisco and nominated conservative Senator Barry M. Goldwater, of Arizona for President, and Congressman William E. Miller of New York for Vice-President. The conservative platform called for victory in foreign affairs and less government spending.

July 18- August 30	Negro riots caused by ghetto living took place in Harlem (July 18-22), Rochester (July 24-25), Jersey City (August 2-4), Chicago (August 16-17), and Philadelphia (August 28-30).
July 21	Announced his disapproval of the riots in New York City, and offered federal assistance to the Mayor of New York in investigating these disturbances.
July 30	Approved the Organization of American States' decision on Cuban aggression against Venezuela. Cuba was condemned for its actions.
August 3	Instructed Navy to take retaliatory action in the Gulf of Tonkin as a result of a North Vietnamese attack upon the U.S. destroyer Maddox on August 2.
August 5	Sent Special Message to Congress on United States policy in Southeast Asia which pledged United States support for peace and security in Southeast Asia. United States planes bombed torpedo boat bases in North Vietnam.
August 7	Praised Congress for its Joint Resolution concerning the Gulf of Tonkin incident. The Resolution pledged united determination to take all necessary measures in support of freedom, and in defense of peace, in Southeast Asia.
August 20	Signed the Economic Opportunity Act providing for an initial expenditure of $1 billion for such varied programs as the Job Corps, VISTA, Work Study, and Community Action.
August 26	Left for the Democratic National Convention in Atlantic City, where he was nominated for the Presidency. Accepted Hubert Humphrey as Vice-Presidential running mate. The platform included a strong civil rights plank.
August 27	Delivered his acceptance speech before the National Convention at Atlantic City, and called for the passage and implementation of his progressive programs.

September 2   Signed the Housing Act providing for urban and rural renewal programs to alleviate blight and assure lasting beauty.

September 3   Accepted resignation of Attorney General Robert F. Kennedy. Strained relations existed between the two men since the 1960 Democratic Convention.

September 5   Announced the successful construction of the new Polaris A-3 missile, and the development of a long-lived nuclear reactor.

September 7-17   Made a campaign tour which took him to ten states in the West and along the Pacific Coast.

Although Johnson made a few campaign trips, in general, the campaign was a poor one. Johnson stood on his record and said nothing that would antagonize anyone. His strategy was to win over as many Republican moderates as possible, and a number of prominent businessmen threw their support to him. Labor and the Negro vote was his as well. Goldwater attacked "peaceful co-existence," and the moral decay of America.

September 24 Ordered publication of the findings of the Warren Commission on the assassination of President Kennedy.

October 5   Sent message to the Second Conference of nonaligned nations meeting in Cairo asking for their cooperation in maintaining peace throughout the world.

October 15   In the Soviet Union, Khrushchev was replaced by Leonid Brezhnev, who became Party Secretary, and by Alexsei Kosygin, who became Premier.

October 16   Announced the confirmation of the first Chinese nuclear device of low yield.

October 25   Issued Executive Order establishing the Federal Development Planning Committee for Appalachia.

November 4   Johnson and Humphrey defeated Republican candidates Senator Barry Goldwater of Arizona and Representative William Miller of New York in a landslide. The popular vote was 41.9 million for Johnson and 26.4 million for Goldwater; the electoral margin was 486 to 52.

November 16   Appointed Gardner Ackley as Chairman and Arthur Okun as a member of the Council of Economic Advisers.

December 4   Approved Civil Rights regulations covering the programs of Federal departments and agencies. These prohibited discrimination in these offices.

December 7-8   Met with new Prime Minister of Great Britain, Harold Wilson, for talks on the Middle East, Europe and the Far East. Both nations reaffirmed their determination to support the peacekeeping operations of the United Nations.

December 16   Accepted resignation of Luther Hodges as Secretary of Commerce, effective January 15, 1965. Appointed John Connor as new Secretary of Commerce also effective as of January 18, 1965.

December 18   Announced decision to build a sea level canal and to negotiate a new treaty with Panama.

1965

January 4   Delivered State of the Union Address in which he detailed his "Great Society" proposals for the nation.

January 12-13   Met with Prime Minister Eisaku Sato of Japan for talks concerned with arms control, a total nuclear test ban, and other defense arrangements.

January 20   Johnson was inaugurated and delivered a short inaugural address stressing his new program for "The Great Society," which included a voting rights bill, aid to schools, immigration law reform, and an attack on disease.

SECOND TERM

February 2   Sent Special Message to Congress requesting home rule for the District of Columbia.

February 7   Ordered withdrawal of American dependents from South Vietnam. The Viet Cong attacked United States forces at Pleiku, and Johnson ordered U.S. air raids on North Vietnam. The bombing of North Vietnam continued on a regular basis, while the United States presented evidence of North Vietnamese infiltration of South Vietnam.

February 8 Sent Special Message to Congress on conservation and the restoration of the nation's natural beauty.

February 13 Attended swearing in of Nicholas Katzenbach as Attorney General and William Ramsey Clark as Deputy Attorney General.

February 18 Martin Luther King led a non-violent voter registration drive in Selma, Alabama. Sheriff Jim Clark prevented the Negroes from entering the Selma courthouse to register. Two thousand Negroes were arrested, unarmed demonstrators were clubbed, and a young Negro woodcutter was killed.

March 2 Sent Special Message to Congress on the "Nation's Cities." Called for a Department of Housing and Urban Development.

March 3 Johnson's Appalachian Program went into effect. It authorized $1.1 billion to fight poverty in an eleven state area.

March 15 Gave television message to the nation on civil rights. He told the American people that he wanted "to be the President who helped to end war among the brothers of this earth."

March 16 Signed a bill establishing Goddard Day in honor of the father of modern rocketry. In a rush to emulate Roosevelt's "one hundred days," Johnson attempted to push through Congress dozens of major bills. His actions bogged down in the Spring of 1965, and he did not come close to the Roosevelt record. His total record for 1965, however, was very impressive. One hundred and fifteen bills, not counting appropriations bills, were sent to Congress. Of these, ninety were signed into law.

March 23 Spoke by telephone with Gus Grissom and John Young following the successful orbital flight of Gemini 3.

March 26 Announced, on television, the arrest of various Ku Klux Klan members by the F.B.I. These Klansmen were charged with the murder of Mrs. Viola Luizzo in Alabama. Johnson called the Klan "a hooded society of bigots."

March 30   Issued statement on the bombing of the U.S. Embassy in Saigon.

March 31   Accepted resignation of C. Douglas Dillon as Secretary of the Treasury. Appointed Henry H. Fowler to fill the vacancy on April 1, 1965.

April 7   Made major foreign policy address at Johns Hopkins University concerning Vietnam. The address was entitled "Peace without Conquest." Announced that the United States was ready to start "unconditional discussions" to end the war.

April 8   North Vietnam announced the peace conditions it would consider in ending the war. They included: withdrawal of U.S. troops; the end of foreign bases in Vietnam; recognition of the National Liberation Front in South Vietnam; and reunification of Vietnam without foreign interference.

April 11   Signed the Elementary and Secondary Education Bill at Johnson City, Texas. It provided aid to school districts with a large number of poor families, and authorized grants to states to purchase school materials for pupils in public and private, including parochial, schools. During the first year, over $1 billion was spent by the government in this area.

April 24   Civil War broke out in the Dominican Republic between the Dominican Revolutionary Party under Juan Bosch, and military conservatives led by General Elias Wessin y Wessin. The conservatives eventually succeeded in ousting Bosch and his group from power.

April 28   Attended swearing in ceremonies of Admiral William F. Raborn and Richard Helms as Director and Deputy Director of the C.I.A.

            Ordered American troops into the Dominican Republic to protect American life and property, and to prevent a Communist takeover. O.A.S. organized a peace force to join the United States troops.

May 1   Ordered additional American forces into the Dominican Republic, and announced that he would give full support to the operations of the Organization of American States in the troubled island.

May 11   Signed proclamation adding Ellis Island to the Liberty Island National Monument.

May 14   Communist China exploded a second atomic bomb.

May 18   Called for repeal of Section 14b of the Taft-Hartley Labor Law which permitted states to pass "right to work" laws. Nineteen states had passed such laws. Repeal of 14b passed the House on July 28, but was blocked by the Senate.

May 27   Sent Special Message to Congress on "Reorganization Plans for the Executive Branch of the government."

June 1   Ordered the withdrawal of U.S. Marines from the Dominican Republic.

June 4   Delivered the commencement address at Howard University. Johnson's topic was Civil Rights and the speech was entitled "To Fulfill These Rights."

June 19   A military regime under Nguyen Cao Ky was established in South Vietnam.

June 21   Signed Excise Tax Reduction Bill which reduced excise taxes on furs, playing cards, jewelry, etc., by some $4 billion.

June 30   Signed bill limiting duty-free imports by tourists. The amount per tourist was reduced to $100.

July 3   Ordered further withdrawal of U.S. forces from the Dominican Republic.

July 20   Appointed Arthur J. Goldberg as U.S. Ambassador to the United Nations. Assumed position on July 26.

July 27   Appointed John W. Gardner as the new Secretary of Health, Education and Welfare to replace Anthony J. Celebrezze who was appointed Judge of the U.S. Court of Appeals of the Sixth Circuit on the same day. Assumed position on August 18.

July 28   Sent letter to Secretary General U-Thant emphasizing U.S. willingness to negotiate on Vietnam. Went on T.V. to explain his "moderate" position on Vietnam to the nation.

July 30	Signed Medicare Bill in the Truman Library in Independence, Missouri, as part of the Social Security laws. The bill had been sponsored by Congressman Wilbur D. Mills of Arkansas.
August 6	Signed Voting Rights Act eliminating literary tests and other restrictive registration devices that had been designed to keep Negroes from the polls.
August 10	Signed the Housing and Urban Development Act providing for a $30 million rent subsidy for low income families.
August 11-15	Riots broke out in the Watts district of Los Angeles.
August 15	Offered any and all Federal assistance to cities or states hit by riots. This statement came at the conclusion of the Watts riots in Los Angeles, California.
August 24	Appointed Judge Thurgood Marshall as Solicitor General.
August 29	Spoke on the telephone with astronauts Gordon Cooper and Charles Conrad following the successful completion of the Gemini 5 mission.
September 1	Announced that agreement had been reached with the O.A.S. on forming a new government in the Dominican Republic.
September 3	Announced on a television broadcast the settlement of the steel dispute.
September 4	Recognized the new government in the Dominican Republic.
September 5	President Charles DeGaulle of France insisted that NATO withdraw all troops and bases from France by 1967.
September 9	Signed Bill establishing a Department of Housing and Urban Development.
October 3	Signed Immigration Bill at Liberty Island, New York City. The Bill ended the 1924 nation-origins quota system. Immigration would now be based on the occupational needs of the United States.
October 4	Appointed Abe Fortas of Texas to the Supreme Court.

October 8   Underwent surgery for removal of gall-bladder at Bethesda Naval Hospital, Maryland. Released from hospital on October 21.

October 22   Signed Highway Beautification Act, which provided generous compensation to outdoor advertisers and junk yard owners to remove their unsightly properties. This was Johnson's present to Lady Bird, and he was furious with anyone who had opposed the passage of the bill.

November 3   Announced that the United States would participate in the Buenos Aires meeting of the Inter-American Economic and Social Council. Appointed Lawrence F. O'Brien as Postmaster General.

November 8   Signed the Higher Education Act of 1965 at Southwest Texas State College. The Act provided a three year $23 billion program of Federal scholarships to needy students and a college building construction grant.

November 20   The number of United States troops killed in Vietnam since 1961 reached 1,095.

December 24   Ordered a halt to the bombing of North Vietnam.

December 31   Denounced proposed price increase by the Bethlehem Steel Company.

1966

January 12   Delivered State of the Union Address. It was a short, dull message, primarily concerned with foreign policy.

January 18   Attended swearing in ceremonies for Robert C. Weaver and Robert C. Wood as Secretary and Under Secretary of Housing and Urban Development. Weaver was the first Negro to serve in the Cabinet.

January 19   Asked Congress for $12.8 billion additional for the war in Vietnam.

January 24   Sent Congress a record budget of $112.9 billion for fiscal 1967 to be used to wage war in Vietnam and to build the "Great Society."

January 27   Senator J. William Fulbright, a close Johnson friend, who opposed the war in Vietnam, began a series of hearings before the Senate Foreign Relations Committee on the war. A great debate ensued in the United States over the American role in Vietnam as statesmen and citizens divided into "Hawks" (those supporting intervention to stop the spread of Chinese Communism in Southeast Asia), and "Doves" (those who opposed the war as a threat to world peace).

January 31   Announced resumption of air strikes on North Vietnam.

February 6-8   Met with Lieutenant General Nguyen Van Thieu (Chief of State) and Lieutenant General Nguyen Cao Ky (Prime-Minister) of South Vietnam at Honolulu to discuss the problems of the Vietnamese war. With the Vietnamese leaders, Johnson issued the Declaration of Honolulu which declared their determination to defend South Vietnam against aggression, and their commitment to the search for a just peace.

March 1   Attended swearing in ceremonies of Jack H. Vaughn as Director of the Peace Corps.

March 3   Signed "Cold War G.I. Bill of Rights."

March 28-29   Met with Prime-Minister Indira Gandhi of India for talks concerning economic aid. Agreed to a $2 million food shipment to famine-hit India.

April 10   Signed bill authorizing an official residence for the Vice-President.

May 6   Announced the formation of the Demonstration Cities Program. Federal funds were to be used to help cities rebuild and restore large areas of slums and blight to decent living sections.

May 21   Sent additional troops to Thailand to prevent Communist infiltration.

May   Stokely Carmichael, President of the Student Non-Violent Coordinating Committee (SNCC), introduced the concept of a unified Negro community with the phrase "Black

Power." Negro leaders throughout the country split over the acceptance of this new concept.

June 2   Sent message of congratulations to NASA following the successful landing of Surveyor I on the moon.

Joaquin Balaguer, a rightist, defeated the leftist, Juan Bosch, and became President of the Dominican Republic.

June 6   NATO officially moved its headquarters to Belgium.

James Meredith, the first Negro student to ever attend the University of Mississippi (1962), was wounded by a sniper while making a "march against fear" in rural Mississippi.

June 13   The Supreme Court in Miranda vs. Arizona ruled that statements made by a prisoner under interrogation could not be used as evidence unless legal safeguards were used in obtaining them.

June 28   Removed last United States troops from the Dominican Republic.

June 29   Met with Prime-Minister Harold E. Holt of Australia for talks concerning Vietnam situation. Ordered bombing attacks on the oil installations of Haiphong and Hanoi.

June 30   Appointed Richard Helms as Director of the Central Intelligence Agency.

July 1   France officially removed its troops from NATO.

July 29   Announced that a favorable agreement had been reached in the airline strike.

August 2   Issued statement on the need for an effective firearms control act.

August 6   Daughter Luci Baines married Patrick Nugent at the Shrine of the Immaculate Conception in Washington, D.C.

August 10   The Red Guard Movement, which armed its Chinese youth to maintain the ideals of the Communist Revolution began. Mao Tse-tung continued to hold his power in China despite widespread opposition.

August 14   Met with General William Westmoreland for talks on Vietnam at the L.B.J. Ranch in Texas.

September 8   Signed Urban Mass Transportation Act.

September 11   South Vietnam held elections for an assembly to draft a new constitution. Despite the terrorist tactics of the Viet Cong, 81 percent of the registered voters went to the polls.

September 14-15   Met with President Ferdinand E. Marcos of the Philippines for a cordial exchange of views on international developments of common significance.

October 7   Delivered a speech at the National Conference of Editorial Writers in New York City, replacing Secretary of State Dean Rusk who was unable to appear. Johnson called for "peaceful engagement" between the United States and the Soviet Union despite their severe differences over Vietnam.

Met with U-Thant of Burma, Secretary General of the United Nations, at the U.N. building in New York City. Asked Thant to obtain Ho Chi Minh's agreement to negotiate the war. Also insisted that Thant accept United States promotion for a second term as Secretary General even though Thant argued that he was tired and wanted to retire.

October 10   Met with Soviet Foreign Minister Andrei Gromyko at the White House, where discussions on Vietnam were held. Johnson vehemently argued the United States case in Vietnam while Gromyko repeated the Soviet complaint that a settlement was impossible as long as American planes were bombing North Vietnam.

October 11   Announced forthcoming meeting between Washington, London, and Bonn on military security in Central Europe. The meeting began on October 20, 1966.

October 15   Signed bill creating a Department of Transportation.

October 17-November 2   President Johnson undertook a seventeen day Asian-Pacific trip to discuss the Vietnam situation and other related matters with American allies in the East. He visited Hawaii, American Samoa, New Zealand, Malaysia, South

Korea, and Alaska. The highlight of the trip was a summit meeting of most Southeast Asian leaders at Manila at which the seven nations at the conference committed themselves to securing the freedom of Vietnam (October 23-25).

October 26   Visited United States troops in Vietnam, which at that time numbered about 400,000. American casualties by this date stood at 44,402, of which 6,664 were dead.

November 3   Signed Demonstration Cities Bill and the Clean Water Restoration Bill.

November 4   Signed the new Minimum Wage Act which increased the minimum wage to $1.40 an hour and covered 8,000,000 additional workers.

November 16   Underwent surgery to repair a defect at the site of the incision made during his gall-bladder operation at Bethesda Naval Hospital, Maryland.

November 19   Left hospital and went to the L.B.J. Ranch in Texas for convalescence following operation. Returned to Washington on November 25.

November 29   Announced a cutback in Federal spending for the current fiscal year.

December 2-4   Escalated the fighting in Vietnam by ordering heavy air strikes on Hanoi. This was the first time the North Vietnamese capital had been bombed since June 29.

December 8   Announced that agreement had been reached among United Nations members on an Outer Space Treaty.

December 24   Ordered a three day Christmas truce in the Vietnam fighting.

December 31   At the end of 1966, the legislative output for that year totaled 1,001 bills passed, and 66,289 Johnson appointments confirmed. Yet, few of the measures passed pertained to the "Great Society." A pall seemed to have settled over the nation as a result of Johnson's continued escalation of the war in Vietnam.

1967

January 11	Delivered State of the Union Address. This message again repeated his stand on Vietnam and his proposals for the "Great Society."
January 13	Asked for a record administrative budget of $135 billion for fiscal, 1968.
January 15-16	Ordered new air strikes on Hanoi. These strikes were followed by White House assurances that the civilian populations had not been bombed, and these assurances were followed by admissions that some civilians might have perished "by accident" in the attacks on military targets.
	Appointed Alan S. Boyd as Secretary of Transportation.
January 27	The United States, Great Britain, and the Soviet Union signed a pact barring nuclear weapons in space.
February 2	Sent letter to Ho Chi Minh requesting direct peace discussions. However, at the same time, he stated that the bombings would continue until a matching "de-escalation" was made by North Vietnam.
February 6	Met with Robert F. Kennedy at the White House to discuss Kennedy's recent European tour. A garbled story had leaked to the press which rumored that Kennedy was returning from Paris with a firm peace proposal from North Vietnam. In a wild 45 minute meeting, Senator Kennedy (he had been elected to the Senate from New York in 1965) denied having leaked any peace plan story to the press. Johnson demanded that Kennedy hold a press conference, and declare that no peace offer had ever been made. Kennedy refused to do so.
February 8	Announced a four day cease-fire in Vietnam in honor of the Tet (lunar New Year) holiday. Johnson expressed his hope that the cease-fire might be extended into peace negotiations.
February 11	The states ratified the Twenty-Fifth Amendment to the Constitution, which established the conditions, and the order of Presidential succession in the case of Presidential disability.
February 14	Ordered the resumption of bombing raids on North Viet-

nam, and further escalated the war by signaling the American Command in Thailand to bomb Hanoi from Thai bases.

February 15   Ho Chi Minh replied to Johnson's letter of February 2. He proclaimed his unwillingness to accept the status of aggressor in the conflict, and turn over South Vietnam to the United States. He repeated the conditions for peace negotiations that had been stated by his Foreign Minister.

February 15   Sent Special Message to Congress on the "Need for Further Civil Rights Legislation" in which he called for equal justice for all Americans, and measures to end housing discrimination. No legislation in this area was passed.

February 21   Sent Message to the Geneva Disarmament Conference assuring non-nuclear nations that their development of nuclear energy for peaceful purposes would not be hindered by accepting the treaty against the spread of nuclear weapons.

March 1   Appointed Ramsay Clark, Attorney General of the United States.

March 6   Sent Special Message to Congress on Selective Service. Asked for increased monthly quotas, and stated that "Freedom's Glory was Freedom's Price."

March 14   In a Special Message to Congress on "Urban and Rural Poverty," he exhorted the legislators to finish "America's unfinished business."

March 16   Appointed Ellsworth Bunker Ambassador to South Vietnam.

Delivered speech before the Tennessee Legislature in Nashville in which he tried to justify his stand on Vietnam, and the resumption of the bombing raids.

March 19-22   Undertook trip to Guam for a Vietnam War Conference with "his Generals" and Premier Ky. Much of the discussion was given over to what General Westmoreland considered an essential escalation in troop numbers above the 475,000 scheduled to be on hand toward the end of the year.

March 30   Appointed William McChesney Martin Chairman of the Federal Reserve Board.

March 31	NATO withdrew all troops and bases from France.
April 12-14	Met with Latin American leaders at the Western Hemisphere Summit Conference in Punta del Este, Uruguay. Cuba was not represented.
April 14	Offered United States aid to Latin American governments if they honored their commitments to establish a Latin American Common Market and to cooperate in other economic ventures.
April 24	Flew to Bonn, West Germany, to attend funeral of former Chancellor Conrad Adenauer.
April 25-26	Conferred with West German and other European leaders including Charles de Gaulle in Bonn, concerning Vietnam, Berlin, and other world problems.
May 15	Fifty nations, including the United States, and the European Common Market members signed an agreement which reduced tariffs by about one-third. International financial negotiations had been taking place in Geneva since 1963 (The Kennedy Round).
May 18	Secretary General U-Thant honored Egypt's request by ordering the withdrawal of United Nations' troops from the Egyptian-Israeli border. Frequent border skirmishes had been taking place, and tensions in the Middle East had reached a boiling point.
May 22	The United Arab Republic began a blockade of the Strait of Tiran, at the mouth of the Gulf of Aqaba, preventing Israeli ships from leaving the port of Eilath, Israel's only outlet to the Red Sea.
May 23	Appointed Alexander B. Trowbridge as Secretary of Commerce.
May 24	Advocated United Nations mediation in the Arab-Israeli Conflict.
May 25	Sent Special Message to Congress on the "Political Process in America," in which he recommended changes and reform in political campaigns.

May 26   Flew to Montreal, Canada, to tour Expo-67, and then went on to Ottawa for talks with Canadian Prime-Minister Lester Pearson.

June 5   War broke out in the Middle East between Israel and Egypt, Jordan and Syria. The Soviets supported the Arabs with armaments and diplomatic encouragement, while the United States took a neutral position despite Johnson's earlier assurances of aid to Israel in event of war. However, the American position of neutrality was looked upon by the Arab states as one in support of Israel.

June 7   Praised United Nations Security Council Resolution proposing a cease-fire in the Mid-East.

The three day Middle Eastern war ended, after Israel had completely routed the Arab forces, and occupied large chunks of Arab territory, including the remainder of the divided city of Jerusalem. Israel pledged she would never again relinquish Jerusalem nor the Jordanian territory on the East bank of the Jordan River. The General Assembly of the United Nations met in emergency session in an attempt to settle the war, but was not able to exert any decisive influence on the outcome of the conflict.

June 14   Appointed Soliciter General Thurgood Marshall to the Supreme Court. He was the first Negro to serve on the Supreme Court of the United States.

June 22   Daughter Luci gave birth to grandson, Patrick Lyndon Nugent.

June 23 & 25   Held Summit Conference with Premier Alexei Kosygin of the Soviet Union at Glassboro State College in New Jersey for far-ranging discussions, concerned with the bases of world tensions.

July 11   Secretary of Defense Robert McNamara returned to the United States after a five day trip to Vietnam. He conferred with Johnson, and severely criticized General Westmoreland's handling of the war. Johnson stoutly defended Westmoreland, and ordered McNamara to prepare a statement for reporters declaring that everything was going well in the political, economic, and military situations in Vietnam.

McNamara complied with the President's order.

July 12-27   Severe Negro riots broke out in Newark, New Jersey (July-12-17), and in Detroit, (July 23-27), leaving 63 dead and scores injured. In the period 1964-1967, outbreaks of racial violence rocked 50 United States cities.

July 23   Ordered Federal troops into riot torn Detroit to help curb the disorders.

July 24   In a television address to the American people, Johnson urged all citizens to condemn and combat lawlessness throughout the nation.

July 27   Appointed Special Advisory Committee on Civil Disorders to probe urban race riots and recommend remedial measures. Governor Otto Kerner of Illinois was appointed Chairman of the Committee, and Mayor John V. Lindsay of New York, Deputy Chairman.

August 3   Requested Congress to enact a ten percent income tax surcharge to help combat inflation. Chairman Wilbur Mills of the House Ways and Means Committee killed Johnson's request for 1967.

August 24   Hailed U.S.-U.S.S.R. draft of a nuclear non-proliferation treaty as a great gift to future generations.

September 3   South Vietnam held elections for a civil government, and elected Nguyen Van Thieu as President, and Nguyen Cao Ky as Vice-President.

September 29   After having been attacked by Senator Thruston Morton of Kentucky for his "bankrupt" Vietnam policy, Johnson made the "San Antonio Declaration" before the National Legislative Conference meeting in San Antonio. He said that the United States was willing to stop all aerial and naval bombardment of North Vietnam, when such cessation would lead promptly to productive discussions. This cryptic statement meant very little since Johnson still refused to accept the Hanoi conditions for peace negotiations.

October 13   By Executive Order, Johnson extended protection against job discrimination in the Federal government and its private contractors to women.

November 3 Established an Advisory Panel on urban disorder entitled the INS in Riot Affected Areas Committee, and appointed Governor Richard J. Hughes of New Jersey as Chairman.

November 10 Offered to meet with Hanoi leaders on a neutral ship on a neutral sea if it would spur a settlement in the Vietnam War.

November 18 Promised not to devaluate the U.S. dollar, despite the British devaluation of the pound sterling, as a financial crisis was beginning to develop throughout all of Europe.

November 28 Announced that Secretary of Defense Robert McNamara would be leaving the Cabinet to become the President of the International Bank for Reconstruction and Development.

December 2 Pledged that the United States, under the terms of the nuclear non-proliferation treaty, would permit international inspection of all U.S. nuclear facilities except those with direct national defense significance.

December 8 Daughter Lynda Bird married Captain Charles S. Robb in a White House ceremony. Johnson was the first President to give away two daughters while in the White House.

December 20-21 Flew to Australia to attend memorial services for Prime-Minister Holt who had been lost in a swimming accident.

December 21 Met with heads of government of other nations who had contributed troops to the Vietnam War.

December 22 Met with South Vietnamese President Nguyen Van Thieu for talks in Canberra, Australia.

December 23 Visited United States troops at Camranh Bay, South Vietnam for one and three quarters hours. Then flew to Pakistan where he met with Ayub Kahn in Karachi, and continued his trip to Rome where he had an hour and a quarter audience with Pope Paul VI. He also conferred with President Saragat and other Italian officials. Returned home on December 24.

December 28 Ordered a cease-fire in Vietnam in honor of the Tet New Year holidays.

1968

January 2	Asked Americans to defer "non-essential" travel outside of the Western Hemisphere for two years. Johnson said that he would weigh legislation to limit travel and spending abroad in order to cut the international payments deficit by $500 million. He also announced that he was considering ways to interest Europeans in traveling to the United States.
January 3	Senator Eugene McCarthy of Wisconsin announced his candidacy for the Democratic Presidential nomination, and stated that he would enter the New Hampshire primary.
January 5	Johnson came under mounting pressure from Congress to halt the war against North Vietnam in order to test Hanoi's latest offer to begin peace talks.
January 7-8	Held talks with Prime Minister Levi Eshkol of Israel at the L.B.J. Ranch. Eshkol was given permission to buy American Phantom fighter-bombers and Skyhawks if he would praise Johnson's war in Vietnam, and pledge resistance to aggression wherever it occurred.
January 17	Delivered State of the Union Address. The speech was primarily concerned with the American Commitment in Vietnam, and was received by Congress without much enthusiasm.
January 19	Appointed Clark Clifford, Secretary of Defense.
January 23	North Korean patrol boats captured the 83 crew members and the *U.S.S. Pueblo,* an electronic spyship, off the North Korean coast near Wonsan. The *Pueblo* had roamed these waters for a month to locate the position, and determine the strength of North Korean radar installations.
January 24	Sent Special Message to Congress on additional civil rights legislation, especially in the field of open housing.
January 25	Called up 14,787 Air Force and Naval Reservists to active duty as a result of the *Pueblo* seizure. Johnson stated that this action was precautionary.
January 26	In a televised speech to the nation, Johnson reported the *Pueblo* capture, and urged the North Koreans to release the ship and its crew. North Korea refused to do until the

United States admitted it had been spying.

January 29 Called off the Tet cease-fire because of massive enemy buildup in the Northern provinces. The bombing pause of North Vietnam was not affected.

January 30 During the Tet holiday, the Viet Cong mounted major offensives in three-fourths of the forty four provincial capitals of South Vietnam. These offensives were coordinated with Viet Cong and North Vietnamese attacks which had begun toward the end of 1967. The Tet offensive also concentrated on military headquarters and strategic locations. The American embassy in Saigon was occupied by the Viet Cong, and stone by stone, the ancient Imperial City of Hue was smashed. To make matters worse, the spector of another Dien Bien Phu arose at Khesanh, a strategic American base in the Ashow Valley, where North Vietnamese troops surrounded thousands of American troops, who could be supplied only by air. In the serious Khesanh situation, Johnson made the Joint Chiefs sign a guarantee that Khesanh could be held, and told them "I don't want another damned Dien Bien Phu." American forces held out at Khesanh until they were suddenly ordered to abandon the base several months later.

February 1 Richard M. Nixon formally announced his candidacy for President.

February 8 Former Governor of Alabama, George C. Wallace, announced his candidacy for the office of President, and the formation of a third party.

February 13 Ordered the sending of 10,500 more troops to South Vietnam to cope with the stepped-up enemy offensive.

February 16 Appointed C.R. Smith, Secretary of Commerce.

February 20 The Senate Foreign Relations Committee, under Senator Fulbright, began an examination of the Gulf of Tonkin incidents. Former Secretary of Defense McNamara testified, and assured the Committee that United States destroyers had come under attack by the North Vietnamese naval vessels.

February 22   Fulbright accused Johnson and McNamara of telling only one side of the story about the Gulf of Tonkin action.

February 24   Allied forces retook the Imperial Palace in Hue, as fighting in that beleagured city had just about come to a close. Khesanh had not been relieved, although reenforcements had been dispatched to this base. The Tet offensives had just about run their courses, but it had required a large sacrifice of American ground forces, and, in the process of retaking the attacked cities, American air might had destroyed most of them.

February 28   Governor George Romney of Michigan, who had declared his candidacy for the Presidency early in 1967, announced his withdrawal from the race after having been beaten badly in the New Hampshire Republican primary by Nixon. His incoherent position on the war, and his "brainwashed" statements concerning his trip to South Vietnam, finished him as a candidate long before the primary.

March 11-12   Secretary of State Rusk testified before the Senate Foreign Relations Committee on foreign aid, but Senator Fulbright used the occasion to challenge the Administration's Vietnam policy.

March 12   Senator McCarthy won the New Hampshire Democratic Presidential primary. He captured 20 out of the 24 delegates, and received forty percent of the vote. Johnson received 26,337 write-in votes, but finished a poor second.

March 14   A run on the gold markets in Europe imperiled the dollar, as well as the post-war international exchange system. Congress removed the 25 percent gold cover for United States dollars in circulation. On the request of the United States, Great Britain closed the London gold market, while the central bankers of the international gold pool met at Washington, and established a tenuous double standard for gold transactions abroad. France refused to go along with this plan, and continued to sell and buy gold. The Federal Reserve Board raised the United States discount rate from 4½ to 5 percent in an effort to strengthen the dollar and curb inflationary pressure.

March 16   Kennedy announced his candidacy for the Democratic Presidential nomination at a press conference in Washington. He said that in order to change United States policy in Vietnam, the nation must change the men directing that policy.

March 18   In a speech before the National Farmers Union in Minneapolis, Minnesota, Johnson called for austerity, and total national effort to win the war in Vietnam, and to solve the nation's domestic problems.

March 20   Johnson's National Advisory Commission on Civil Disorders presented its report after eight months of work. Johnson received the report without much enthusiasm, and showed little inclination toward implementing the Commission's recommendations for a massive effort to bring domestic peace, and end the two-race society in the United States. The press, across the country, sharply criticized him for his attitude.

March 22   Appointed Wilbur J. Cohen, Secretary of Health, Education and Welfare.

Appointed Sargent Shriver, Ambassador to France.

Announced his intention to remove Westmoreland as Commander of United States forces in Vietnam, and appoint him Chief of Staff sometime before July 2.

March 23   Czechoslovakian Communist Party Chief Alexander Dubcek, and Premier Josef Lenart conferred with Soviet Party Chief Leonid Brezhnev, Soviet Premier Kosygin, Polish Party Chief Vladimir Gomulka, East German Chancellor Walter Ulbricht, and other Communist leaders, to allay Communist Bloc fears that the Czechoslovakian liberalization drive would endanger her adherence to common policies. Difficulties, however, continued during the next few months.

March 31   In a televised speech to the nation, Johnson announced that he had ordered a halt to the bombing of ninety percent of North Vietnam, and invited North Vietnamese leaders to join him in a series of mutual moves toward peace negotiation. He also announced that he would not seek nor would he accept the nomination of the Democratic Party for reelection.

April 1   Explained decision not to seek reelection in a speech before the National Association of Broadcasters in Chicago. His primary reason for not running, he said, was to save the integrity of the office of President.

April 4   Dr. Martin Luther King Jr. was murdered by a sniper in Memphis, Tennessee. The assassin, James Earle Ray, was arrested in London several months later. That evening, Johnson decried this act of violence in a nationally televised speech. He also announced that he had postponed his trip to Honolulu for talks concerning Vietnam and Korea because of Dr. King's death.

April 4-6   Proclaimed a National Day of Mourning for Dr. King. Riots broke out in 125 cities in the aftermath of the King Assassination. Forty five persons were killed, 2,600 were injured, and 21,000 were arrested. Johnson ordered the mobilization of Federal troops to deal with the rioting in the nation's capital, and in Chicago, Major Richard J. Daley issued an order to the Chicago police to "shoot to kill any arsonist —shoot to cripple or maim anyone looting."

April 7   North Vietnam agreed to establish contacts with the United States as a preliminary to peace talks.

April 9   Martin Luther King was buried in South View Cemetery in Atlanta, Georgia. His casket was carried through the streets of Atlanta in a crude farm wagon pulled by two Georgia mules. Johnson did not attend the funeral, but sent Vice President Humphrey in his place.

April 10   Appointed Marvin Watson, Postmaster General.

April 11   Signed Civil Rights Act of 1968 which was mainly concerned with open housing. The Bill, which Johnson dedicated to the memory of Dr. King, barred discrimination in 80 percent of the nation's housing.

April 15-16 Met with President Park and Pacific Military Commanders in Hawaii for discussions concerning Korea and Vietnam. At a press conference following the meeting, he urged

North Vietnamese leaders to match his efforts to arrange a meeting of Ambassadors in a neutral capital as a first step toward peace negotiations. Returned home on April 17.

April 19 North Vietnam announced that its choice of a site for peace negotiations was Warsaw. Hanoi rejected all other sites including the ten that Secretary Rusk had proposed the preceding day.

April 23 Students for a Democratic Society (SDS) at Columbia University in New York led a violent demonstration to protest the University's proposed construction of a new gymnasium on the site of a park in Harlem. Members of the Harlem community joined the protestors, led by Mark Rudd, head of SDS at Columbia. Police were eventually brought in to clear the campus resulting in a violent confrontation between students and police. Columbia students then led a strike which closed down the university for more than a month. The action at Columbia began a long series of student protests and strikes at other colleges and universities across the nation.

April 26 A giant anti-war rally took place in New York. 200,000 students in the New York metropolitan area cut classes to participate in the marches and demonstrations culminating in an 87,000 person rally in Central Park's Sheep Meadow.

April 27 Vice-President Humphrey announced that he would seek the Democratic nomination for President. Johnson endorsed Humphrey, although he did not actively campaign for him.

April 29 Accepted the resignation of Arthur J. Goldberg, the United States Ambassador to the United Nations.

May 2 What began on March 22 as a minor clash between protesting French students and police at suburban Nanterre University grew into a national uprising. All classes at Nanterre and Paris University were suspended after repeated student agitation. Armed riot police evicted hundreds of left wing student demonstrators from the Sorbonne.

Reverend Ralph D. Abernathy began the massive "invasion" of Washington, D.C. by poor people from all over the nation to demonstrate for economic reforms and improvements.

The aim was to set up a shantytown in the nation's capital, and to remain there until the Congress met the demands of the poor people. "Resurrection City," as the camp was titled, suffered from internal dissension, poor leadership, inadequate funds, and public indifference. After several months, the camp was disbanded, and its inhabitants slowly filtered back to their own homes, most of their demands not met by the legislators.

May 3   Announced that the United States and North Vietnam had agreed to begin formal peace talks in Paris on May 10 or soon thereafter. Johnson expressed the hope that the agreement represented a move toward peace, but cautioned the nation about the hazards and difficulties that lay ahead.

May 4   Appointed W. Averell Harriman as Chief United States negotiator in Paris, and Cyrus Vance as the number two man for the discussions.

May 5   Urged Speaker of the House John McCormick of Massachusetts to enact the ten percent income tax surcharge as soon as possible.

May 7   Robert Kennedy won the Indiana Democratic Presidential Primary gathering 42 percent of the vote. Governor Roger D. Branigan received 31 percent of the vote, while Senator Eugene McCarthy finished third getting 27 percent of the vote. It was Kennedy's first primary victory.

May 8   Signed Federal School Lunch Program Bill.

May 9   Thousands of students in Paris clashed with French riot police. On May 11, eight million workers, half of the labor force in France, went out on strike in support of the students. Many occupied their factories, and marched with the students in Paris chanting, "DeGaulle adieu." The students, led by twenty-three year old Daniel Cohn Bendit, (Danny the Red), continued the demonstrations as the Latin Quarter became a battleground. DeGaulle, however, rallied the nation by warning, "Without me France would collapse." He called for a June referendum on the main issues of the student-worker revolt, and stated that if he did not receive a vote of confidence from the nation, he would resign.

May 12   Vietnam peace talks began in Paris. Harriman and Vance represented the United States, while Xuan Thuy and Ha Van Lao spoke for North Vietnam. The South Vietnamese government refused to send a delegation to the peace discussions. Agreement between the United States and North Vietnam stalled as North Vietnam demanded an unconditional halt to United States bombing, a guarantee the United States was not willing to give.

May 29   Eugene McCarthy won the Oregon Democratic Presidential Primary getting 45 percent of the vote. Kennedy received 39 percent, Johnson 13 percent and Humphrey 3 percent.

June 4   Kennedy won the California Democratic Presidential Primary with 46 percent of the vote. He also was the winner in the South Dakota primary with 50 percent of the vote.

June 5   Senator Kennedy was murdered in Los Angeles, California, by a Jordanian immigrant Sirhan Bishara Sirhan. In a televised speech to the nation, Johnson pleaded with Americans to put an end to violence. He also asked Congress for strong gun control legislation.

Named Special Presidential Committee to study the reasons for violence in the United States, and appointed Dr. Milton Eisenhower its Chairman.

Spoke at the Glassboro State College Commencement in New Jersey, and invited the Soviet Union to join the United States in a global peacemaking effort. He also suggested some of the areas of cooperation. Premier Kosygin subsequently turned down Johnson's offer.

June 6   Proclaimed a National Day of Mourning for Senator Kennedy.

June 8   Attended Kennedy memorial services at St. Patrick's Cathedral in New York City. Then, flew back to Washington, where several hours later he met the Kennedy funeral train, and attended the burial of Senator Kennedy at Arlington National Cemetery.

June 12   Hailed United Nations General Assembly approval of the Nuclear Non-Proliferation Treaty, and stated that this approval obligated the United States and the Soviet Union to move rapidly on other disarmament negotiations.

June 13 Made another appeal for U.S.-U.S.S.R. cooperation at the White House ceremony marking the formal ratification of the U.S.-U.S.S.R. Consular Treaty.

June 19 Signed Wiretapping Bill, which made certain forms of telephone "snooping" legal.

June 23 In the June referendum and election in France, President DeGaulle won a landslide victory which gave the Gaullists solid control of the National Assembly. DeGaulle promised the students that he would enact the most sweeping reforms since Napoleon. The workers received generous raises, which helped bring on a monetary crisis for France later in the year.

June 24 Sent Special Message to Congress proposing tighter controls on firearms.

June 26 Accepted resignation of Chief Justice of the Supreme Court, Earl Warren, and announced the appointment of Associate Justice Abe Fortas to this post. To fill the vacancy created by Fortas' appointment, he named an old friend, Homer Thornberry, as Associate Justice.

June 27 Sent Special Message to Congress proposing a Constitutional Amendment that would lower the voting age to eighteen.

June 28 Signed the ten percent income tax surcharge rise, and the Federal spending cut package.

July 1 Attended White House ceremony at the signing of the Nuclear Non-Proliferation Treaty. Announced an American-Soviet accord on starting talks aimed at limiting and reducing offensive nuclear weapons, and defensive anti-missile systems. The United States, Great Britain, and the Soviet Union, and 58 other nations were signatories of the treaty.

July 2 The Biafran Relief Committee announced that more than one million more people would die in Biafra before the end of

August, if that region did not receive twenty times as much aid as it was currently receiving. The Nigerian Civil War, which began when the Ebo dominated Biafran province seceded from Nigeria in 1967, became a war of mass starvation. Throughout 1968, various nations made attempts to airlift food. At the year's end, Johnson offered eight cargo planes to carry food into Biafra from neutral bases, but the hungry continued to die.

July 3　　Entertained forty Latin American diplomats at the L.B.J. Ranch in Texas.

July 4　　With the forty diplomats, Johnson toured HemisFair 68 in San Antonio, Texas.

July 5-8　　Visisted Salvador, Costa Rica, Guatamala, Honduras, and Nicaragua, meeting with the leaders of these nations individually and collectively to discuss hemispheric problems. The meetings proved to be quite successful in improving United States relations in Central America.

July 9　　Returned to the L.B.J. Ranch after having dropped off Central American Presidents, via Air Force I, in their respective countries.

July 18-20　　Met with President Thieu of South Vietnam in Honolulu for talks concerning the war, as well as the peace discussions taking place in Paris. Thieu again balked at sending a delegation to the talks, as a result of Hanoi's insistence upon accepting the N.L.F. as an equal partner at the discussions.

July 26　　Signed the Conservation and Beautification Bill, which marked the fiftieth bill he had signed in the field of conservation and the preservation of natural beauty during his administrations. He gave the pens that he had used in signing all of these bills as mementos to Mrs. Johnson, and to Secretary of the Interior Stewart Udall.

July 29　　Pope Paul VI issued his encyclical concerning birth control entitled "Humanae Vitae." It stated, "Conforming to the fundamental principles of human and Christian vision of marriage, we must once again state that there must be excluded absolutely, as a licit way in which to regulate births, the direct interruption of the generative process." The Pope's encyclical caused widespread protest in the United States, and in other countries throughout the world.

August 3   The continuing Czechoslovakian liberalization campaign led by the reformist Alexander Dubcek continued to frighten the Soviet Union and the other Communist states in Europe. A Communist Summit Conference was held at Bratislava to iron out the points of difference between Czechoslovakia, the Soviet Union and the other Soviet bloc nations.

August 5-8   The National Republican Convention meeting in Miami, Florida, nominated Richard M. Nixon for President, and Spiro T. Agnew of Maryland for Vice-President.

August 8   White House officials announced that President Johnson was suffering from diverticulosis, an intestinal ailment.

August 19   In a speech before the Veterans of Foreign Wars meeting in Detroit, Johnson ruled out any change in Vietnam policy for the remainder of his term.

August 20   Two hundred thousand Warsaw Pact troops slammed past border check points and invaded Czechoslovakia. Students jeered, wept, and hurled stones at the invading troops, but hundreds of T-54 Russian tanks rolled into Prague, and the Czech liberalization drive was over.

Johnson called the National Security Council into session to discuss the Soviet invasion of Czechoslovakia. The results of these talks were not disclosed to the public.

August 26-30   The Democratic National Convention met in Chicago and nominated Hubert Humphrey for President and Senator Edmund G. Muskie of Maine for Vice President. Riots and street fighting erupted between thousands of demonstrators who had come to Chicago to protest the war in Vietnam, and to support Senator McCarthy's candidacy, and the Chicago police. Scores were injured and arrested, while a considerable amount of damage was done to the city.

August 29   Announced that he would not go to Chicago to address the Convention because of the dissension, and because of the police and mob violence in the streets. At the same time, he ordered the President's Commission on Violence to probe the causes and events of the disturbances in Chicago.

September 18 President Diaz Ordaz of Mexico ordered federal troops to invade the university in Mexico City, after militant students, who had been protesting government repressive measures since mid-summer, occupied and closed down the National University. Two weeks of fire bombing, sniping, and mass arrests followed. The violence reached its climax, when, in early October, the troops assaulted a student rally killing 33 and wounding 500.

September 25 A Senate filibuster on the nomination of Abe Fortas to Chief Justice began. Fortas was called unfit, and charges of "cronyism" were leveled against Johnson.

September 26 United Nations Ambassador George W. Ball resigned. Johnson replaced him with James Russell Wiggins.

September 27 Signed Federal Water Supply Bill, making Federal funds available to states for the improvement of the water supply networks.

October 2 Having failed to secure Senate confirmation of Abe Fortas' appointment as Chief Justice, Johnson accepted Fortas' request to withdraw his nomination, and did so. The appointment of the new Chief Justice would be left to Johnson's successor.

October 3 George Wallace chose General Curtis E. Le May as his Vice Presidential running mate on the American Independence Party. LeMay, at a press conference, accepted, and stated that he would use nuclear weapons in Vietnam if necessary, but said that he didn't think it would be necessary at this time.

October 10 Announced that he would make no further appointments to the Supreme Court.

In a radio speech, Johnson urged all Democrats to unite behind Humphrey and Muskie, and strongly attacked Nixon, and especially Agnew.

October 11-22 Apollo 7 space capsule was successfully launched and returned to earth. Johnson sent a congratulatory message to the three astronauts; Walter Schirra, Don Eisile, and Walter Cunningham, who had made this spectacular space voyage.

October 24   Lynda Bird Robb gave birth to a daughter named Lucinda at Bethesda Naval Hospital, Maryland.

October 28   Announced he would teach a series of seminars at Rice University in Texas during the Spring of 1969.

October 29   Met with Vietnam commander General Creighton W. Abrams in Washington for strategy talks.

October 30   General Abrams told President Johnson that he could accept military consequences of a complete bombing halt under the present battlefield conditions.

October 31   Announced halt to all United States bombing of North Vietnam. At this same time, he assured South Vietnamese that he would continue to oppose a coalition government being forced upon them.

November 5   Nixon and Agnew defeated Humphrey and Muskie in the Presidential election. The popular vote ended up in a near dead heat, prompting criticism of the electoral college system, and the voicing of proposals for a new presidential election format.

November 23   Following the student unrest, and the worker's strikes in France, a financial crisis ensued in France and the Franc began to flutter. However, President DeGaulle, refused to devaluate the Franc, imposed strong economy measures, and would not allow the Franc to fall.

November 24   In a personal message to DeGaulle, Johnson pledged full United States cooperation in stemming the French financial crisis, which, by November 25, had subsided considerably.

November 26   The South Vietnamese government announced that it was finally sending a delegation to the peace negotiations in Paris. Nguyen Cao Ky was appointed to oversee, and control the Saigon delegation. The N.L.F. had earlier sent Mrs. Nguyen Thi Binh, once a Saigon math teacher, to represent it in Paris.

December 1   The National Committee on the Causes and Prevention of
Violence issued its report entitled "Rights in Conflict." This
report primarily dealt with the riots and violence in Chicago
during the National Democratic Convention. It condemned
the Chicago police, and termed the police attacks as "gratui-
tous, ferocious, and mindless," amounting to what could
be called a "police riot." Johnson's reaction to the Commission's findings was less than enthusiastic.

December 9   The Saigon peace talks delegation arrived in Paris. However,
the South Vietnamese refused to accept any negotiations
in which the N.L.F. was considered an equal participant.
The various contending parties could not agree on who would
talk to whom, or even where each might sit at what sort of
table. As they squabbled the year ran out, and with it the
Johnson Administration's hope of achieving a settlement.
It would not be until 1969, when the Nixon Administration
was about to take over the reigns of government, that the
contending parties finally agreed on the shape of the negotiations table. But, the settlement of peace proceeded very
slowly.

December 13   Met with President Ordaz of Mexico at the El Paso, Texas—
Juarez, Mexico Border Bridge to mark the shifting of the Rio
Grande River into a new channel to form the new Mexican-
American border.

December   Contracted a severe case of the flu, and was hospitalized at
18-22   Bethesda Naval Hospital for several days.

December   In an historic space voyage an American spaceship, Apollo
21-27   8, was put in a lunar orbit and circled the moon ten times
before being successfully brought back to earth. The three
astronauts aboard, Frank Borman, James A. Lovell Jr.,
and William Anders, had seen sights that no other men
had ever seen, and were even able to send back a series of
television "shows" reporting their observations to the
American public.

December 22   The 82 crewmen of the ship *Pueblo*, which had been seized
in January, 1968, were released by the North Koreans after
United States representatives deliberately signed what they
termed as a false confession of espionage inside North
Korean territorial waters in order to bring about the

release. Johnson hailed the release of the *Pueblo's* crew in a public announcement to the nation.

December 25   At the Athens, Greece, airport, an Israeli El Al jetliner was fired upon by several Arab gunmen of the El Fata terrorist group, sparking new outbreaks in the already troubled Middle East.

December 28   As a result of the December 25 attack at the Athens airport, Israeli paratroopers retaliated by attacking the Beiruit airport in Lebanon, and destroying eight aircraft. The Security Council was called into special session to discuss the violent outbreaks in the troubled Middle East, which seemed to be again on the verge of war.

December 29   Premier Kosygin of the Soviet Union sent Johnson a letter setting forth a proposal for a Mid-East peace.

1969

January 10   Announced that he would leave the Soviet proposal on a Mid-East peace to the Nixon Administration.

January 13   Sent Message to Congress requesting an extension of the surtax at the ten percent level for fiscal 1969.

January 14   Delivered final State of the Union Address, which was also a farewell address to the American people. In the speech, Johnson reviewed the accomplishments of his five years in office, and called upon the new administration to carry forward the goals of the "Great Society." While this speech was remarkably free of patriotic oratory concerning Vietnam, the President did pay tribute to the troops fighting in Vietnam, and concluded his address: "I hope it may be said a hundred years from now that by working together we helped to make our country more just—That's what I hope. But I believe that at least it will be said that we tried."

January 20   Richard M. Nixon was inaugurated thirty-seventh President of the United States. After attending a private luncheon in the home of Clark Clifford, Johnson left Washington for his Texas ranch via Air Force I. On his arrival in Austin, he was met by a fairly large and enthusiastic crowd. Lyndon Johnson was home and retired.

ADDRESS BEFORE A JOINT SESSION OF CONGRESS
November 27, 1963

Five days after the assassination of President John F. Kennedy, Lyndon Johnson went before a joint session of Congress and delivered, what may be called, his "First Inaugural Address." He pledged to continue the Kennedy Administration's programs

. . . . All I have I would have given gladly not to be standing here today.

The greatest leader of our time has been struck down by the foulest deed of our time. Today John Fitzgerald Kennedy lives on in the immortal words and works that he left behind. He lives on in the mind and memories of mankind. He lives on in the hearts of his countrymen.

No words are sad enough to express our sense of loss. No words are strong enough to express our determination to continue the forward thrust of America that he began.

The dream of conquering the vastness of space — the dream of partnership across the Atlantic — and across the Pacific as well — the dream of a Peace Corps in less developed nations — the dream of education for all of our children — the dream of jobs for all who seek them and need them — the dream of care for our elderly — the dream of an all-out attack on mental illness — and above all, the dream of equal rights for all Americans, whatever their race or color — these and other American dreams have been vitalized by his drive and by his dedication.

And now the ideas and the ideals which he so nobly represented must and will be translated into effective action.

Under John Kennedy's leadership, this Nation has demonstrated that it has the courage to seek peace, and it has the fortitude to risk war. We have proved that we are a good and reliable friend to those who seek peace and freedom. We have shown that we can also be a formidable foe to those who reject the path of peace and those who seek to impose upon us or our allies the yoke of tyranny.

This 'Nation will keep its commitments from South Viet-Nam to West Berlin. We will be unceasing in the search for peace; resourceful in our pursuit of areas of agreement even with those with whom we

71

differ; and generous and loyal to those who join with us in common cause.

In this age when there can be no losers in peace and no victors in war, we must recognize the obligation to match national strength with national restraint. We must be prepared at one and the same time for both the confrontation of power and the limitation of power. We must be ready to defend the national interest and to negotiate the common interest. This is the path that we shall continue to pursue. Those who test our courage will find it strong, and those who seek our friendship will find it honorable. We will demonstrate anew that the strong can be just in the use of strength; and the just can be strong in the defense of justice. . . .

We will serve all the Nation, not one section or one sector, or one group, but all Americans. These are the United States – a united people with a united purpose. . . .

An assassin's bullet has thrust upon me the awesome burden of the Presidency. I am here today to say I need your help; I cannot bear this burden alone. I need the help of all Americans, and all America. This Nation has experienced a profound shock, and in this critical moment, it is our duty, yours and mine, as the Government of the United States, to do away with uncertainty and doubt and delay, and to show that we are capable of decisive action; that from the brutal loss of our leader we will derive not weakness, but strength; that we can and will act and act now.

From this chamber of representative government, let all the world know and none misunderstand that I rededicate this Government to the unswerving support of the United Nations, to the honorable and determined execution of our commitments to our allies, to the maintenance of military strength second to none, to the defense of the strength and the stability of the dollar, to the expansion of our foreign trade, to the reinforcement of our programs of mutual assistance and cooperation in Asia and Africa, and to our Alliance for Progress in this hemisphere.

On the 20th day of January, in 1961, John F. Kennedy told his countrymen that our national work would not be finished "in the first thousand days, nor in the life of this administration, nor even perhaps in our lifetime on this planet. But," he said, "let us begin."

Today, in this moment of new resolve, I would say to all my fellow Americans, let us continue.

This is our challenge—not to hesitate, not to pause, not to turn about and linger over this evil moment, but to continue on our course so that we may fulfill the destiny that history has set for us. Our most immediate tasks are here on this Hill. . . .

First, no memorial oration or eulogy could more eloquently honor President Kennedy's memory than the earliest possible passage of the civil rights bill for which he fought so long. We have talked long enough in this country about equal rights. We have talked for one hundred years or more. It is time now to write the next chapter, and to write it in the books of law.

I urge you again, as I did in 1957 and again in 1960, to enact a civil rights law so that we can move forward to eliminate from this Nation every trace of discrimination and oppression that is based upon race or color. There could be no greater source of strength to this Nation both at home and abroad.

And second, no act of ours could more fittingly continue the work of President Kennedy than the early passage of the tax bill for which he fought all this long year. This is a bill designed to increase our national income and Federal revenues, and to provide insurance against recession. . . .

In short, this is no time for delay. It is a time for action — strong, forward-looking action on the pending education bills to help bring the light of learning to every home and hamlet in America — strong, forward-looking action on youth employment opportunities; strong, forward-looking action on the pending foreign aid bill, making clear that we are not forfeiting our responsibilities to this hemisphere or to the world, nor erasing Executive flexibility in the conduct of our foreign affairs — and strong, prompt, and forward-looking action on the remaining appropriation bills. . . .

As one who has long served in both Houses of the Congress, I firmly believe in the independence and the integrity of the legislative branch. And I promise you that I shall always respect this. It is deep in the marrow of my bones. With equal firmness, I believe in the capacity and I believe in the ability of the Congress, despite the division of opinions which characterize our Nation, to act — to act wisely, to act vigorously, to act speedily when the need arises.

The need is now. I ask your help.

We meet in grief, but let us also meet in renewed dedication and renewed vigor. Let us meet in action, in tolerance, and in mutual understanding. John Kennedy's death commands what his life conveyed — that America must move forward. The time has come for Americans of all races and creeds and political beliefs to understand and to respect one another. So let us put an end to the teaching and the preaching of hate and evil and violence. Let us turn away from the fanatics of the far left and the far right, from the apostles of bitterness and bigotry, from those defiant of law, and those who pour venom into our Nation's bloodstream.

I profoundly hope that the tragedy and the torment of these terrible days will bind us together in new fellowship, making us one people in our hour of sorrow. So let us here highly resolve that John Fitzgerald Kennedy did not live – or die – in vain.

APPOINTMENT OF THE WARREN COMMISSION
November 30, 1963

In the national shock after Dallas, Johnson appointed a Commission under Chief Justice Earl Warren to investigate his predecessor's assassination. The Commission reported in 1964 that the murderer was Lee Harvey Oswald.

PURSUANT to the authority vested in me as President of the United States, I hereby appoint a Commission to ascertain, evaluate, and report upon the facts relating to the assassination of the late President John F. Kennedy and the subsequent violent death of the man charged with the assassination. The Commission shall consist of –

The Chief Justice of the Junited States, Chairman; Senator Richard B. Russell; Senator John Sherman Cooper; Congressman Hale Boggs; Congressman Gerald R. Ford; The Honorable Allen W. Dulles; The Honorable John J. McCloy.

The purpose of the Commission are to examine the evidence developed by the Federal Bureau of Investigation and any additional evidence that may hereafter come to light or be uncovered by Federal or State authorities; to make such further investigation as the Commission finds desirable; to evaluate all the facts and circumstances surrounding such assassination, including the subsequent violent death of the man charged with the assassination, and to report to me its findings and conclusions.

The Commission is empowered to prescribe its own procedures and to employ such assistants as it deems necessary.

Necessary expenses of the Commission may be paid from the "Emergency Fund for the President."

All Executive departments and agencies are directed to furnish the Commission with such facilities, services, and cooperation as it may request from time to time.

LYNDON B. JOHNSON

The White House
November 29, 1963

ON THE HIGHER EDUCATION FACILITIES ACT
December 16, 1963

Instrumental in the passage of this very important measure aiding Higher Education were Congressman Adam Clayton Powell, and Senator Wayne Morse.

I am proud and happy to approve at this time the Morse-Green bill, the Higher Education Facilities Act of 1963, and to especially compliment Chairman Powell, Congresswoman Green, and their colleagues in the House, Senator Morse and his colleagues in the Senate, and everyone else who worked so hard for the passage of this very important legislation. . . .

Working together, the Congress and the executive branch have made possible the enactment of a series of legislative landmarks in the field of education. Under these various measures:

1. We will help to provide college classrooms for several hundred thousand more students who will nearly double college enrollment in this decade.

2. We will help to build 25 to 30 new public community colleges every year.

3. We will help to construct the technical institutes that are needed to close the gap in this crucial area of trained manpower.

4. We will help to build graduate schools and facilities in at least 10 to 20 major academic centers.

5. We will help to improve the quality of library facilities in our own universities and colleges.

6. We will increase the number of medical school graduates and we will relieve the growing shortages of physicians and dentists and other needed professional health personnel.

7. We will enable some 70,000 to 90,000 additional students to attend college each year under an expanded loan program.

8. We will modernize and expand our Federal-State programs for vocational education in order to train for the changing world of work the 8 out of 10 young people who will never obtain a college education.

9. We will reduce the shortage of qualified personnel for the training and teaching of mentally retarded and other handicapped children.

10. We will expand our manpower development and training program to meet the growing problem of untrained, unemployed school dropouts.

11. We will expand programs for teaching science and mathematics and foreign languages, while extending the other valuable provisions of the National Defense Education Act.

12. We will continue the program of Federal financial assistance for the construction and the maintenance and the operation of schools that are crowded by the presence of the children of Federal personnel.

13. And finally, we will, under legislation to be passed shortly, provide public libraries for the residents of cities and counties all over this great country who now have only antiquated library facilities and some have no libraries at all.

This legislation is dramatic, and it is concrete evidence of a renewed and continuing national commitment to education as the key to our Nation's social and technological and economic and moral progress. It will help meet the demands of our economy for more skilled personnel; it will enable many more of our young people to cope with the explosion of new knowledge and to contribute effectively in a world of intellectual, political, and economic complexity.

But these new measures will still not do the whole job of extending educational opportunities to all who want and can benefit by them, nor in meeting our growing national needs. I, therefore, strongly urge the Congress to take early, positive action on the unfinished portion of the National Education Improvement Act, particularly those programs which will assist elementary and secondary schools. In addition, I urge prompt action on proposed programs for combating adult illiteracy, for expanding adult education, for improving the quality of education at all levels.

President Kennedy fought hard for this legislation. No topic was closer to his heart. No bill was the object of more of his attention. Both his life and his death showed the importance and the value of sound education. The enactment of this measure is not only a monument to him, it is a monument to every person who participated in passing it and most of you are in this room today.

ADDRESS BEFORE THE GENERAL ASSEMBLY OF THE UNITED NATIONS
December 17, 1963

Johnson went before the United Nations to assure it of the continued cooperation, and active participation of the United States. He emphasized collective security and disarmament.

. . . . We meet in a time of mourning, but in a moment of rededication. My Nation has lost a great leader. This organization has lost a great friend. World peace has lost a great champion.

But John F. Kennedy was the author of new hope for mankind, hope which was shared by a whole new generation of leaders in every continent, and we must not let grief turn us away from that hope. He never quarreled with the past. He always looked at the future. And our task now is to work for the kind of future in which he so strongly believed.

I have come here today to make it unmistakably clear that the assassin's bullet which took his life did not alter his Nation's purpose.

We are more than ever committed to the rule of law, in our own land and around the world.

We believe more than ever in the rights of man, all men of every color, in our own land and around the world.

And more than ever we support the United Nations as the best instrument yet devised to promote the peace of the world and to promote the well-being of mankind. . . .

Like all human institutions, the United Nations has not achieved the highest of hopes that some held at its birth. Our understanding of how to live, live with one another, is still far behind our knowledge of how to destroy one another. . . .

But as our problems have grown, this Organization has grown, in numbers, in authority, in prestige, and its member nations have grown with it, in responsibility and in maturity.

We have seen too much success to become obsessed with failure.

The peace-keeping machinery of the United Nations has worked in the Congo, in the Middle East, and elsewhere.

The great transition from colonial rule to independence has been largely accomplished.

The Decade of Development has successfully begun. The world arms race has been slowed. The struggle for human rights has been gaining new force.

And a start has been made in furthering mankind's common interest in outer space—in scientific exploration, in communications, in weather forecasting, in banning the stationing of nuclear weapons, and in establishing principles of law.

I know that vast problems remain, conflicts between great powers, conflicts between small neighbors, disagreements over disarmament, persistence of ancient wrongs in the area of human rights, residual problems of colonialism, and all the rest. But men and nations, working apart, created these problems, and men and nations working together must solve them.

They can solve them with the help of this Organization, when all members make it a workshop for constructive action, and not a forum for abuse; when all members seek its help in settling their own disputes as well as the disputes of others; when all members meet their financial obligations to it; and when all members recognize that no nation and no party and no single system can control the future of man. . . .

My friends and fellow citizens of the world, soon you will return to your homelands. I hope you will take with you my gratitude for your generosity in hearing me so late in the session. I hope you will convey to your countrymen the gratitude of all Americans for the companionship of sorrow which you shared with us in your messages of the last few weeks. And I hope that you will tell them that the United States of America, sobered by tragedy, united in sorrow, renewed in spirit, faces the New Year determined that world peace, civil rights, and human welfare become not an illusion but a reality.

Man's age old hopes remain our goal: that this world, under God, can be safe for diversity, and free from hostility, and a better place for our children and for all generations in the years to come. And therefore any man and any nation that seeks peace, and hates war, and is willing to fight the good fight against hunger and disease and ignorance and misery, will find the United States of America by their side, willing to walk with them, walk with them every step of the way.

STATE OF THE UNION ADDRESS
January 8, 1964

In his first State of the Union Message, Johnson called for a direct attack on poverty as an essential feature of his domestic program. He urged Congress to proceed on all fronts in the endeavor to make equal opportunity a reality.

. . . . Let this session of Congress be known as the session which did more for civil rights than the last 100 sessions combined; as the session which enacted the most far-reaching tax cut of our time; as the session which declared all-out war on human poverty and unemployment in these United States; as the session which finally recognized the health needs of all of our older citizens; as the session which reformed our tangled transportation and transit policies; as the session which achieved the most effective efficient foreign aid program ever, and as the session which helped to build more homes and more schools and more libraries and more hospitals than any single session of Congress in the history of our republic. . . .

This budget, and this year's legislative program, are designed to help each and every American citizen fulfill his basic hopes. . . .

No single piece of legislation, however, is going to suffice:

We will launch a special effort in the chronically distressed areas of Appalachia.

We must expand our small but our successful area redevelopment program.

We must enact youth employment legislation to put jobless, aimless, hopeless youngsters to work on useful projects.

We must create a National Service Corps to help the economically handicapped of our own country, as the Peace Corps now helps those abroad.

We must modernize our unemployment insurance and establish a high-level commission on automation. If we have the brain power to invent these machines, we have the brain power to make certain that they are a boon and not a bane to humanity.

We must extend the coverage of our minimum wage laws to more than 2 million workers now lacking this basic protection of purchasing power.

We must, by including special school aid funds as part of our education program, improve the quality of teaching and training and counseling in our hardest-hit areas.

We must build more libraries in every area, and more hospitals and nursing homes under the Hill-Burton Act, and train more nurses to staff them.

We must provide hospital insurance for our older citizens, financed by every worker and his employer under Social Security contributing no more than $1 a month during the employe's working career to protect him in his old age in a dignified manner, without cost to the Treasury, against the devastating hardship of prolonged or repeated illness.

We must, as a part of a revised housing and urban renewal program, give more help to those displaced by slum clearance; provide more housing for our poor and our elderly, and seek as our ultimate goal in our free enterprise system a decent home for every American family.

We must help obtain more modern mass transit within our communities as well as low-cost transportation between them.

Above all, we must release $11 billion of tax reduction into the private spending stream to create new jobs and new markets in every area of this land. . . .

In 1963, for the first time in history, we crossed the 70 million job mark, but we will soon need more than 75 million jobs.

In 1963, our gross national product reached the $600 billion level, $100 billion higher than when we took office. But it easily could, and it should, be still $30 billion higher today than it is.

Wages and profits and family income are also at their highest level in history, but I would remind you that 4 million workers and 13 per cent of our industrial capacity are still idle today.

We need a tax cut now to keep this country moving. . . .

Let me make one principle of this Administration abundantly clear. All of these increased opportunities in employment and education, in housing and in every field must be open to Americans of every color. As far as the writ of Federal law will run, we must abolish not some, but all, racial discrimination. For this is not merely an economic issue, or a social, political or international issue. It is a moral issue, and it must be met by the passage this session of the bill now pending in the House.

All members of the public should have equal access to facilities open to the public.

All members of the public should have an equal chance to vote for public officials and to send their children to good public schools, and to contribute their talents to the public good.

Today Americans of all races stand side by side in Berlin and in Vietnam. They died side by side in Korea. Surely they can work and travel side by side in their own country. . . .

My good friends and my fellow Americans, in these last sorrowful weeks we have learned anew that nothing is so enduring as faith and nothing is so degrading as hate.

John Kennedy was a victim of hate, but he was also a great builder of faith — faith in our fellow Americans, whatever their creed or their color or their station in life; faith in the future of man, whatever his divisions and differences.

This faith was echoed in all parts of the world. On every continent and in every land to which Mrs. Johnson and I traveled, we found faith and hope and love toward this land of America and toward our people.

So I ask you now, in the Congress and in the country, to join with me in expressing and fulfilling that faith, in working for a nation, a nation that is free from want, and a world that is free from hate.

A world of peace and justice and freedom and abundance for our time and for all time to come.

THE WAR ON POVERTY MESSAGE
March 16, 1964

Congress responded warmly to the President's plea for help for all Americans. In this Special Message, he outlined to Congress his program for an all out war on poverty which the legislators eventually enacted.

We are citizens of the richest and most fortunate nation in the history of the world. .·. .

The path forward has not been an easy one. — But we have never lost sight of our goal: an America in which every citizen shares all the opportunities of his society, in which every man has a chance to advance his welfare to the limit of his capacities. . . .

There are millions of Americans — one-fifth of our people — who have not shared in the abundance which has been granted to most of us, and on whom the gates of opportunity have been closed.

What does this poverty mean to those who endure it?

It means a daily struggle to secure the necessities for even a meager existence. It means that the abundance, the comforts, the opportunities they see all around them are beyond their grasp. . . .

Our tax cut will create millions of new jobs-new exits from poverty.

If we can raise the annual earnings of 10 million among the poor by only $1,000, we will have added $14 billion a year to our national output. In addition, we can make important reductions in public assistance payments which now cost us $4 billion a year, and in the large costs of fighting crime and delinquency, disease and hunger. . . .

Because it is right, because it is wise, and because, for the first time in our history, it is possible to conquer poverty, I submit, for the consideration of the Congress and the country, the Economic Opportunity Act of 1964. . . .

This act provides five basic opportunities.

It will give almost half a million underprivileged young Americans the opportunity to develop skills, continue education, and find useful work.

It will give every American community the opportunity to develop a comprehensive plan to fight its own poverty— and help them to carry out their plans.

It will give dedicated Americans the opportunity to enlist as volunteers in the war against poverty.

It will give many workers and farmers the opportunity to break through particular barriers which bar their escape from poverty.

It will give the entire Nation the opportunity for a concerted attack on poverty through the establishment, under my direction, of the Office of Economic Opportunity, a national headquarters for the war against poverty.

This is how we propose to create these opportunities.

First. We will give high priority to helping young Americans who lack skills, who have not completed their education, or who cannot complete it because they are too poor. . . .

I therefore recommend the creation of a Job Corps, a work-training program, and a work study program.

A new National Job Corps will build toward an enlistment of 100,000 young men. They will be drawn from those whose background, health, and education make them least fit for useful work. Those who volunteer will enter more than 100 camps and centers around the country. . . .

These are not simply camps for the underprivileged. They are new educational institutions, comparable in innovation to the land-grant colleges. Those who enter them will emerge better qualified to play a productive role in American society.

A new national work-training program operated by the Department of Labor will provide work and training for 200,000 American men and women between the ages of 16 and 21. This will be developed through State and local government as non profit agencies. . . .

A new national work-study program operated by the Department of Health, Education, and Welfare will provide Federal funds for part-time jobs for 140,000 young Americans who do not go to college because they cannot afford it.

There is no more senseless waste than the waste of the brainpower and skill of those who are kept from college by economic circumstance. Under this program they will, in a great American tradition, be able to work their way through school.

Second. Through a new community-action program we intend to strike at poverty at its source — in the streets of our cities and on the farms of our countryside among the very young and the impoverished old.

This program asks men and women throughout the country to prepare long-range plans for the attack on poverty in their own local communities.

These plans will be local plans calling upon all the resources available to the community — Federal and State, local and private, human and material. And when these plans are approved by the Office of Economic Opportunity, the Federal Government will finance up to 90 percent of the additional cost for the first 2 years. . . .

Third. I ask for the authority to recruit and train skilled volunteers for the war against poverty.

Among older people who have retired, as well as among the young. Among women as well as men, there are many Americans who are ready to enlist in our war against poverty. . . .

If the State requests them, if the community needs and will use them, we will recruit and train them and give them the chance to serve.

Fourth. We intend to create new opportunities for certain hard-hit groups to break out of the pattern of poverty.

Through a new program of loans and guarantees we can provide incentives to those who will employ the unemployed.

Through programs of work and retraining for unemployed fathers and mothers we can help them support their families in dignity while preparing themselves for new work.

Through funds to purchase needed land, organize cooperatives, and create new and adequate family farms we can help those whose life on the land has been a struggle without hope.

Fifth. I do not intend that the war against poverty become a series of uncoordinated and unrelated efforts — that it perish for lack of leadership and direction.

Therefore this bill creates, in the Executive Office of the President, a new Office of Economic Opportunity. Its Director will be my personal chief of staff for the war against poverty. I intend to appoint Sargent Shriver to this post.

He will be directly responsible for these new programs. He will work with and through existing agencies of the Government.

This program — the Economic Opportunity Act — is the foundation of our war against poverty. . . .

On many historic occasions the President has requested from Congress the authority to move against forces which were endangering the well-being of our country.

This is such an occasion.

On similar occasions in the past we have often been called upon to wage war against foreign enemies which threatened our freedom. Today we are asked to declare war on a domestic enemy which threatens the strength of our Nation and the welfare of our people. . . .

LYNDON B. JOHNSON

ON THE CIVIL RIGHTS ACT
July 2, 1964

Johnson secured Congressional action on Kennedy's Civil Rights program. The new legislation sought to guarantee Negroes the right to vote, access to all public facilities, and equal job opportunities in businesses employing more than twenty-five people.

My fellow Americans:

I am about to sign into law the Civil Rights Act of 1964. . .

It was proposed more than one year ago by our late and beloved President, John F. Kennedy. It received the bipartisan support of more than two-thirds of the members of both the House and the Senate. An overwhelming majority of Republicans as well as Democrats voted for it.

It has received the thoughful support of tens of thousands of civic and religious leaders in all parts of this nation, and it is supported by the great majority of the American people.

The purpose of this law is simple. It does not restrict the freedom of any American as long as he respects the rights of others. It does not give special treatment to any citizen. It does say that those who are equal before God shall now be equal in the polling booths, in the class rooms, in the factories, and in hotels, and restaurants, and movie theatres, and other places that provide service to the public.

I'm taking steps to implement the law under my constitutional obligation to take care that the laws are faithfully executed.

First, I will send to the Senate my nomination of LeRoy Collins to be Director of the Community Relations Service.

Second, I shall appoint an advisory committee of distinguished Americans to assist Governor Collins in his assignment.

Third, I am sending Congress a request for supplemental appropriations to pay for necessary costs of implementing the law and asking for immediate action.

Fourth, already today in a meeting of my Cabinet this afternoon I directed the agencies of this government to fully discharge the new responsibilities imposed upon them by the law and to do it without delay and to keep me personally informed of their progress.

Fifth, I am asking appropriate officials to meet with representative groups to promote greater understanding of the law and to achieve a spirit of compliance.

Its purpose is national not regional. Its purpose is to promote a more abiding commitment to freedom, a more constant pursuit of justice and a deeper respect for human dignity.

We will achieve these goals because most Americans are law-abiding citizens who want to do what is right. This is why the Civil Rights Act relies first on voluntary compliance, then on the efforts of local communities and states to secure the rights of citizens.

It provides for the national authority to step in only when others can not or will not do the job.

This Civil Rights Act is a challenge to all of us to go to work in our communities and our states, in our homes and in our hearts to eliminate the last vestiges of injustice in our beloved country.

So, tonight I urge every public official, every religious leader, every business and professional man, every working man, every housewife — I urge every American to join in this effort to bring justice and hope to all people and to bring peace to our land. . . .

MESSAGE TO CONGRESS FOLLOWING AGGRESSION IN THE GULF OF TONKIN
August 5, 1964

In August, 1964, North Vietnamese gunboats fired on American destroyers in the Tonkin Gulf off the coast of North Vietnam. Johnson ordered aerial retaliation and then asked Congress to give him broad discretionary power to combat communism in Southeast Asia.

Last night I announced to the American people that the North Vietnamese regime had conducted further deliberate attacks against U.S. naval vessels operating in international waters, and that I had therefore directed air action against gunboats and supporting facilities used in these hostile operations. This air action has now been carried out with substantial damage to the boats and facilities. Two U.S. aircraft were lost in the action.

After consultation with the leaders of both parties in the Congress, I further announced a decision to ask the Congress for a resolution expressing the unity and determination of the United States in supporting freedom and in protecting peace in southeast Asia.

These latest actions of the North Vietnamese regime have given a new and grave turn to the already serious situation in southeast Asia. Our commitments in that area are well known to the Congress. They were first made in 1954 by President Eisenhower. They were further defined in the Southeast Asia Collective Defense Treaty approved by the Senate in February 1955.

This treaty with its accompanying protocol obligates the United States and other members to act in accordance with their constitutional processes to meet Communist aggression against any of the parties or protocol states. . . .

In recent months, the actions of the North Vietnamese regime have become steadily more threatening. . . .

As President of the United States I have concluded that I should now ask the Congress, on its part, to join in affirming the national determination that all such attacks will be met, and that the United States will continue in its basic policy of assisting the free nations of the area to defend their freedom.

As I have repeatedly made clear, the United States intends no rashness, and seeks no wider war. We must make it clear to all that the United States is united in its determination to bring about the end of Communist subversion and aggression in the area. We seek the full and effective restoration of the international agreements signed in Geneva in 1954, with respect to South Vietnam, and again in Geneva in 1962, with respect to Laos. . . .

ON THE ECONOMIC OPPORTUNITY ACT
August 20, 1964

Congress responded to President Johnson's request for a war on poverty by passing a broad bill providing for an initial expenditure of one billion dollars. Sargent Shriver was made head of the Office of Economic Opportunity.

Today for the first time in all the history of the human race, a great nation is able to make and is willing to make a commitment to eradicate poverty among its people.

Whatever our situation in life, whatever our partisan affiliation, we can be grateful and proud that we are able to pledge ourselves this morning to this historic course. We can be especially proud of the nature of the commitments that we are making. . . .

The measure before me this morning for signature offers the answer that its title implies — the answer of opportunity. For the purpose of the Economic Opportunity Act of 1964 is to offer opportunity, not an opiate.

For the million young men and women who are out of school and who are out of work, this program will permit us to take them off the streets, put them into work training programs, to prepare them for productive lives, not wasted lives.

In this same sound, sensible, and responsible way we will reach into all the pockets of poverty and help our people find their footing for a long climb toward a better way of life.

We will work with them through our communities all over the country to develop comprehensive community action programs — with remedial education, with job training, with retraining, with health and employment counseling, with neighborhood improvement. We will strike at poverty's roots. . . .

Every dollar authorized in this bill was contained in the budget request that I sent to the Congress last January. Every dollar spent will result in savings to the country and especially to the local taxpayers in the cost of crime, welfare, of health, and of police protection. . . .

Our American answer to poverty is not to make the poor more secure in their poverty but to reach down and to help them lift themselves out of the ruts of poverty and move with the large majority along the high road of hope and prosperity.

The days of the dole in our country are numbered. I firmly believe that as of this moment a new day of opportunity is dawning and a new era of progress is opening for us all. . . .

STATE OF THE UNION ADDRESS
January 4, 1965

After being elected to the Presidency in his own right in 1964, Johnson outlined his vision of what the rich, restless American nation should try to become in the future. This sketch of what he called "The Great Society" emerged in his 1965 State of the Union Address.

We are entering the third century of the pursuit of American Union.

Two hundred years ago, in 1765, nine assembled colonies first joined together to demand freedom from arbitrary power. . . .

And now, in 1965, we begin a new quest for union. We seek the unity of man with the world he has built — with the knowledge that can save or destroy him — with the cities which can stimulate or stifle him — with the wealth and machines which can enrich or meance his spirit. . . .

But the unity we seek cannot realize its full promise in isolation. For today the state of the Union depends, in large measure, upon the state of the world. . . .

We are prepared to live as good neighbors with all, but we canot be indifferent to acts designed to injure our interests, our citizens, or our establishments abroad. The community of nations requires mutual respect. We shall extend it — and we shall expect it. . . .

Yet we still live in a troubled and perilous world. There is no longer a single threat. There are many. They differ in intensity and danger. They require different attitudes and different answers.

With the Soviet Union we seek peaceful understanding that can lessen the danger to freedom.

Last fall I asked the American people to choose that course.

I will carry forward their command.

If we are to live together in peace, we must come to know each other better.

I am sure the American people would welcome a chance to listen to the Soviet leaders on our television — as I would like the Soviet people to hear our leaders.

In Eastern Europe restless nations are slowly beginning to assert their identity. Your Government, assisted by leaders in labor and business, is exploring ways to increase peaceful trade with these countries and the Soviet Union. I will report our conclusions to the Congress.

In Asia, Communism wears a more aggressive face.

Twice in one generation we have had to fight against aggression in the Far East. To ignore aggression would only increase the danger of a larger war.

Our goal is peace in Southeast Asia. That will come only when aggressors leave their neighbors in peace.

But Communism is not the only source of trouble and unrest. There are older and deeper sources – in the misery of nations and in man's irrepressible ambition for liberty and a better life.

With the free republics of Latin America I have always felt – and my country has always felt – special ties of interest and affection. It will be the purpose of this Administration to strengthen these ties.

Together we share and shape the destiny of the New World. In the coming year I hope to pay a visit to Latin America. And I will steadily enlarge our commitment to the Alliance for Progress as the instrument of our war against poverty and injustice in the Hemisphere. . . .

Tonight I would like briefly to explain some of my major recommendations in the three main areas of national need.

First, we must keep our nation prosperous. We seek full employment opportunity for every American. I will present a budget designed to move the economy forward. More money will be left in the hands of the consumer by a substantial cut in excise taxes. We will continue along the path toward a balanced budget and a balanced economy.

I confidently predict – what every economic sign now tells us – the continued flourishing of the American economy. . . .

As pledged in our 1960 and 1964 Democratic platforms, I will propose to Congress changes in the Taft-Hartley Act including section 14-B. I will do so hoping to reduce conflicts that for several years have divided Americans in various states.

In a country that spans a continent modern transportation is vital to continued growth.

I will recommend heavier reliance on competition in transportation and a new policy for our Merchant Marine.

I will ask for funds to study high-speed rail transportation between urban centers. We will begin with test projects between Boston and Washington. On high-speed trains, passengers could travel this distance in less than four hours.

Second, we must open opportunity to all our people.

Most Americans tonight enjoy a good life. But far too many are still trapped in poverty, idleness and fear.

Let a just nation throw open to them the city of promise:

1. To the elderly, by providing hospital care under Social Security and by raising benefit payments to those struggling to maintain the dignity of their later years.

2. To the poor, through doubling the war against poverty this year.

3. To Negro Americans, through enforcement of the Civil Rights Law and elimination of barriers to the right to vote.

4. To those in other lands seeking the promise of America, through an immigration law based on the work a man can do and not where he was born or how he spells his name.

Our third goal is to improve the quality of American life. We begin with learning. Every child must have the best education our nation can provide.

In addition to our existing programs, I will recommend a new program for schools and students with a first-year authorization of one billion, 500 million dollars.

For the pre-school years we will help needy children become aware of the excitement of learning.

For the primary and secondary school years we will aid public schools serving low-income families and assist students in both public and private schools.

For the college years we will provide scholarships to high school students of the greatest promise and greatest need and guaranteed low interest loans to students continuing their college studies.

New laboratories and centers will help our schools lift their standards of excellence and explore new methods of teaching. . . .

Greatness requires not only an educated people but a healthy people.

We already carry on a large program for research and health. . . . New support for medical and dental education will provide the trained men to apply our knowledge.

Community centers can help the mentally ill and improve health care for school-age children from poor families, including services for the mentally retarded. . . .

In our urban areas the central problem today is to protect and restore man's satisfaction in belonging to a community where he can find security and significance. The first step is to break old patterns — to begin to think, work and plan for the development of entire metropolitan areas. We will take this step with new programs of help for basic community facilities and neighborhood centers of health and recreation. New and existing programs will be open to those cities which work together to develop unified long-range policies for metropolitan areas.

We must also make important changes in our housing programs if we are to pursue these same basic goals. A department of housing and urban development will be needed to spearhead this effort in our cities.

Every citizen has the right to feel secure in his home and on the streets of his community. . . . I will soon assemble a panel of outstanding experts to search out answers to the national problem of crime and delinquency.

For over three centuries the beauty of America has sustained our spirit and enlarged our vision. We must act now to protect this heritage. . . .

THE INAUGURAL ADDRESS
January 20, 1965

In a relatively short inaugural address, Johnson again set forth his dreams for "The Great Society." He stated that he hoped that the entire world could develop such a program.

On this occasion the oath I have taken before you and before God is not my alone, but ours together. We are one nation and one people. Our fate as a nation and our future as a people rest not upon one citizen but upon all citizens. That is the majesty and the meaning of this moment. . . .

Ours is a time of change — rapid and fantastic change — bearing the secrets of nature, multiplying the nations, placing in uncertain hands new weapons for mastery and destruction, shaking old values and uprooting old ways. Our destiny in the midst of change will rest on the unchanged character of our people and on their faith. . . .

In a land of great wealth, families must not live in hopeless poverty. In a land rich in harvest, children just must not go hungry. In a land of healing miracles, neighbors must not suffer and die untended. In a great land of learning and scholars, young people must be taught to read and write. . . .

Justice requires us to remember: when any citizen denies his fellow, saying: "His color is not mine or his beliefs are strange and different," in that moment he betrays America, though his forebears created this Nation. . . .

THE WORLD AND CHANGE

The American convenant called on us to help show the way for the liberation of man. And that is today our goal. Thus, if as a nation, there is much outside our control, as a people no stranger is outside our hope.

Change has brought new meaning to that old mission. We can never again stand aside, prideful in isolation. Terrific dangers and troubles that we once called "foreign" now constantly live among us. If American lives must end, and American treasure be spilled, in countries that we barely know, then that is the price that change has demanded of conviction and of our enduring convenant. . . .

How incredible it is that in this fragile existence we should hate and destroy one another. There are possibilities enough for all who will abandon mastery over others to pursue mastery over nature. There is world enough for all to seek their happiness in their own way.

Our Nation's course is abundantly clear. We aspire to nothing that belongs to others. We seek no dominion over our fellow man, but man's dominion over tyranny and misery.

But more is required. Men want to be part of a common enterprise, a cause greater than themselves. And each of us must find a way to advance the purpose of the Nation, thus finding new purpose for ourselves. . . .

Let us now join reason to faith and action to experience, to transform our unity of interest into a unity of purpose. For the hour and the day and the time are here to achieve progress without strife, to achieve change without hatred; not without difference of opinion but without the deep and abiding divisions which scar the union for generations. . . .

THE AMERICAN BELIEF

I do not believe that the Great Society is the ordered, changeless, and sterile battalion of the ants. It is the excitement of becoming — always becoming, trying, probing, falling, resting, and trying again — but always trying and always gaining.

In each generation, with toil and tears, we have had to earn our heritage again. If we fail now then we will have forgotten in abundance what we learned in hardship: that democracy rests on faith, that freedom asks more than it gives, and the judgment of God is harshest on those who are most favored.

If we succeed it will not be because of what we have, but it will be because of what we are; not because of what we own, but rather because of what we believe.

For we are a nation of believers. Underneath the clamor of building and the rush of our day's pursuits, we are believers in justice and liberty and in our own union. We believe that every man must some day be free. And we believe in ourselves.

And that is the mistake that our enemies have always made. In my lifetime, in depression and in war they have awaited our defeat. Each time, from the secret places of the American heart, came forth the faith that they could not see or that they could not even imagine. And it brought us victory. And it will again. . . .

I will repeat today what I said on that sorrowful day in November last year: I will lead and I will do the best I can.

But you, you must look within your own hearts to the old promises and to the old dreams. They will lead you best of all.

ON VIETNAM POLICY
April 7, 1965

At the time of its delivery, this speech was widely taken as an indication of the Johnson Administration's willingness to negotiate a conclusion to the Vietnamese war. Later it became clear that the Administration had consistently passed up opportunities for negotiation.

. . . Over this war, and all Asia, is the deepening shadow of Communist China. The rulers in Hanoi are urged on by Peking. This is a regime which has destroyed freedom in Tibet, attacked India, and been condemned by the United Nations for aggression in Korea. It is a nation which is helping the forces of violence in almost every continent. The contest in Vietnam is part of a wider pattern of aggressive purpose.

Why are these realities our concern? Why are we in South Vietnam? We are there because we have a promise to keep. Since 1954 every American President has offered support to the people of South Vietnam. We have helped to build, and we have helped to defend. Thus, over many years, we have made a national pledge to help South Vietnam defend its independence. And I intend to keep our promise.

To dishonor that pledge, to abandon this small and brave nation to its enemy, and to the terror that must follow, would be an unforgivable wrong.

We are also there to strengthen world order. Around the globe, from Berlin to Thailand, are people whose well-being rests, in part, on the belief that they can count on us if they are attacked. To leave Vietnam to its fate would shake the confidence of all these people in the value of American commitment, the value of America's word. The result would be increased unrest and instability, and even wider war.

We are also there because there are great stakes in the balance. Let no one think for a moment that retreat from Vietnam would bring an end to conflict. The battle would be renewed in one country and then another. The central lesson of our time is that the appetite of aggression is never satisfied. To withdraw from one battlefield means only to prepare for the next. We must say in Southeast Asia, as we did in Europe, in the words of the Bible: "Hitherto shalt thou come, but no further."

There are those who say that all our effort there will be futile, that China's power is such it is bound to dominate all Southeast Asia. But there is no end to that argument until all the nations of Asia are swallowed up.

There are those who wonder why we have a responsibility there. We have it for the same reason we have a responsibility for the defense of freedom in Europe. World War II was fought in both Europe and Asia, and when it ended we found ourselves with continued responsibility for the defense of freedom.

Our objective is the independence of South Vietnam, and its freedom from attack. . . . We will do everything necessary to reach that objective. And we will do only what is absolutely necessary.

In recent months, attacks on South Vietnam were stepped up. Thus it became necessary to increase our response and to make attacks by air. This is not a change of purpose. It is a change in what we believe that purpose requires.

We do this in order to slow down aggression.

We do this to increase the confidence of the brave people of South Vietnam who have bravely borne this brutal battle for so many years and with so many casualties.

And we do this to convince the leaders of North Vietnam, and all who seek to share their conquest, of a very simple fact:

We will not be defeated.

We will not grow tired.

We will not withdraw, either openly or under the cloak of a meaningless agreement. . . .

Once this is clear, then it should also be clear that the only path for reasonable men is the path of peaceful settlement.

Such peace demands an independent South Vietnam securely guaranteed and able to shape its own relationships to all others, free from outside interference, tied to no alliance, a military base for no other country.

These are the essentials of any final settlement.

We will never be second in the search for such a peaceful settlement in Vietnam.

There may be many ways to this kind of peace: in discussion or negotiation with the governments concerned; in large groups or in small ones; in the reaffirmation of old agreements or their strengthening with new ones.

We have stated this position over and over again fifty times and more, to friend and foe alike. And we remain ready, with this purpose, for unconditional discussions.

And until that bright and necessary day of peace we will try to keep conflict from spreading. We have no desire to see thousands die in battle, Asians or Americans. We have no desire to devastate that which the people of North Vietnam have built with toil and sacrifice. We will use our power with restraint and with all the wisdom we can command. But we will use it. . . .

We will always oppose the effort of one nation to conquer another nation. We will do this because our own security is at stake.

But there is more to it than that. For our generation has a dream. It is a very old dream. But we have the power and now we have the opportunity to make it come true.

For centuries, nations have struggled among each other. But we dream of a world where disputes are settled by law and reason. And we will try to make it so. . . .

The ordinary men and women of North Vietnam and South Vietnam — of China and India — of Russia and America — are brave people. They are filled with the same proportions of hate and fear, of love and hope. Most of them want the same things for themselves and their families. Most of them do not want their sons ever to die in battle, or see the homes of others destroyed. . . .

Every night before I turn out the lights to sleep, I ask myself this question: Have I done everything that I can do to unite this country? Have I done everything I can to help unite the world, to try to bring peace and hope to all the peoples of the word? Have I done enough?

Ask yourselves that question in your homes and in this hall tonight. Have we done all we could? Have we done enough? . . .

ON THE ELEMENTARY AND SECONDARY EDUCATION BILL
April 11, 1965

In a one-room tin-roofed Junction School near his birth-place, Johnson signed the $1.344 billion Elementary and Secondary Education Bill, a sweeping measure designed to make Federal funds available to local communities for the improvement of their educational facilities.

I want to welcome to this little school of my childhood many of my former schoolmates and many who went to school with me at Cotulla and Houston and San Marcos, as well as some of my dear friends from the educational institutions of this area.

My Attorney General tells me that it is legal and constitutional to sign that act on Sunday, even on Palm Sunday. My minister assured me that the Lord's day will not be violated by making into law a measure which will bring mental and moral benefits to millions of our young people.

So I have chosen this time and this place for two reasons.

First, I do not wish to delay by a single day the program to strengthen this Nation's elementary and secondary schools. . . .

Second, I felt a very strong desire to go back to the beginnings of my own education — to be reminded and to remind others of that magic time when the world of learning began to open before our eyes. — In this one-room schoolhouse Miss Katie Deadrich taught eight grades at one and the same time. . . .

Over a century and a quarter ago, the President of the Republic of Texas, Mirabeau B. Lamar, proclaimed education as "the guardian genius of democracy . . . . the only dictator that free men acknowledge and the only security that free men desire."

But President Lamar made the mistaken prophecy that education would be an issue "in which no jarring interests are involved and no acrimonious political feelings excited." For too long, political acrimony held up our progress. For too long, children suffered while jarring interests caused stalemate in the efforts to improve our schools. Since 1946 Congress tried repeatedly, and failed repeatedly, to enact measures for elementary and secondary education.

Now, within the past 3 weeks, the House of Representatives, by a vote of 263 to 153, and the Senate, by a vote of 73 to 18, have passed the most sweeping educational bill ever to come before Congress. It represents a major new commitment of the Federal Government to quality and equality in the schooling that we offer our young people. I predict that all of those of both parties of Congress who supported the enactment of this legislation will be remembered in history as men and women who began a new day of greatness in American society.

By passing this bill, we bridge the gap between helplessness and hope for more than 5 million educationally deprived children.

We put into the hands of our youth more than 30 million new books, and into many of our schools their first libraries.

We reduce the terrible timelag in bringing new teaching techniques into the Nation's classrooms.

We strengthen State and local agencies which bear the burden and the challenge of better education.

And we rekindle the revolution – the revolution of the spirit against the tyranny of ignorance.

As a son of a tenant farmer, I know that education is the only valid passport from poverty.

As a former teacher – and, I hope, a future one – I have great expectations of what this law will mean for all of our young people.

As President of the United States, I believe deeply no law I have signed or will ever sign means more to the future of America.

To each and everyone who contributed to this day, the Nation is indebted. . . .

ON AMERICAN INTERVENTION IN THE
DOMINICAN REPUBLIC
May 2, 1965

*Fearing an alleged Communist takeover, and a Civil War
in the Dominican Republic, Johnson ordered American
forces into that country. He was bitterly criticized for this
action, one of the most controversial of his Presidency.*

. . . Last week our observers warned of an approaching political storm in the Dominican Republic. I immediately asked our Ambassador to return to Washington at once so that we might discuss the situation and might plan a course of conduct. But events soon outran our hopes for peace.

Saturday, April 24 — 8 days ago — while Ambassador Bennett was conferring with the highest officials of your Government, revolution erupted in the Dominican Republic. Elements of the military forces of that country overthrew their government. However, the rebels themselves were divided. Some wanted to restore former President Juan Bosch. Others opposed his restoration. President Bosch, elected after the fall of Trujillo and his assassination, had been driven from office by an earlier revolution in the Dominican Republic.

Those who opposed Mr. Bosch's return formed a military committee in an effort to control that country. The others took to the street, and they began to lead a revolt on behalf of President Bosch. Control and effective government dissolved in conflict and confusion. . . .

On Wednesday afternoon there was no longer any choice for the man who is your President. I was sitting in my little office reviewing the world situation with Secretary Rusk, Secretary McNamara, and Mr. McGeorge Bundy. Shorty after 3 o'clock I received a cable from our Ambassador, and he said that things were in danger; he had been informed the chief of police and governmental authorities could no longer protect us. We immediately started the necessary conference calls to be prepared.

At 5'14, almost 2 hours later, we received a cable that was labeled "critic," a word that is reserved for only the most urgent and immediate matters of national security.

The cable reported that Dominican law enforcement and military officials had informed our Embassy that the situation was completely out of control and that the police and the government could no longer give any guarantee concerning the safety of Americans or any foreign nationals.

Ambassdador Bennett, who is one of our most experienced Foreign Service officers, went on in that cable to say that only an immediate landing of American forces could safeguard and protect the lives of thousands of Americans and thousands of other citizens of some 30 other countries. Ambassador Bennett urged your President to order an immediate landing.

In this situation hesitation and vacillation could mean death for many of our people, as well as many of the citizens of other lands.

I thought that we could not and we did not hesitate. Our forces, American forces, were ordered in immediately to protect American lives. They have done that. They have attacked no one, and although some of our servicemen gave their lives, not a single American civilian or the civilian of any other nation, as a result of this protection, lost their lives. . . .

The revolutionary movement took a tragic turn. Communist leaders, many of them trained in Cuba, seeing a chance to increase disorder, to gain a foothold, joined the revolution. They took increasing control. And what began as a popular democratic revolution, committed to democracy and social justice, very shortly moved and was taken over and really seized and placed into the hands of a band of Communist conspirators. . . .

The American nations cannot, must not, and will not permit the establishment of another Communist government in the Western Hemisphere. This was the unanimous view of all the American nations when, in January 1962, they declared, and I quote: "The principles of communism are incompatible with the principles of the Inter-American system.' . . .

To those who fight only for liberty and justice and progress I want to join with the Organization of American States in saying — in appealing to you tonight to lay down your arms and to assure you there is nothing to fear. The road is open for you to share in building a Dominican democracy, and we in America are ready and anxious and willing to help you. Your courage and your dedication are qualities which your country and all the hemisphere need for the future. You are needed to help shape that future. And neither we nor any other nation in this hemisphere can or should take it upon itself to ever interfere with the affairs of your country or any other country.

We believe that change comes, and we are glad it does, and it should come through peaceful process. But revolution in any country is a matter for that country to deal with. It becomes a matter calling for hemispheric action only — repeat, only — when the object is the establishment of a Communist dictatorship.

Let me also make clear tonight that we support no single man or any single group of men in the Dominican Republic. Our goal is a simple one. We are there to save the lives of our citizens and to save the lives of all people. Our goal, in keeping with the great principles of the inter-American system, is to help prevent another Communist state in this hemisphere. And we would like to do this without bloodshed or without large-scale fighting.

The form and the nature of the free Dominican government, I assure you, is solely a matter for the Dominican people. . . .

ON PROJECT HEAD START
May 18, 1965

As another part of his program to improve the quality of American education, and to attack the poverty problem, Johnson pushed through Congress Project Head Start. It was an excellent example of the Federal government's cooperation with local communities.

On this beautiful spring day it is good to be outside in the Rose Garden. Of course, the White House is a place where when you go outside you are still inside.

In that same vein, I would note that the Rose Garden is a garden without roses today, and the Fish Room is now a room without fish. But there is one compensation — open nearly any door here in the West Wing and you are liable to run into Sargent Shriver, and sometimes you will find him in more than one room at the same time.

This is a very proud occasion for him and for us today, because it was less than 3 months ago that we opened a new war front on poverty. We set out to make certain that poverty's children would not be forever-more poverty's captives. We called our program Project Head Start.

The program was conceived not so much as a Federal effort but really as a neighborhood effort, and the response we have received from the neighborhoods and the communities has been most stirring and the most enthusiastic of any peacetime program that I can remember.

Today we are able to announce that we will have open, and we believe operating this summer, coast-to-coast, some 2,000 child development centers serving as many as possibly a half million children.

This means that nearly half the preschool children of poverty will get a headstart on their future. These children will receive preschool training to prepare them for regular school in September. They will get medical and dental attention that they badly need, and parents will receive counseling on improving the home environment.

This is a most remarkable accomplishment and it has been done in a very short time. It would not be possible except for the willing and the enthusiastic cooperation of Americans throughout the country.

I believe this response reflects a realistic and a wholesome awakening in America. It shows that we are recognizing that poverty perpetuates itself.

Five and six year old children are inheritors of poverty's curse and not its creators. Unless we act these children will pass it on to the next generation, like a family birthmark.

This program this year means that 30 million man-years – the combined lifespan of these youngsters – will be spent productively and rewardingly, rather than wasted in tax-supported institutions or in welfare-supported lethargy.

I believe that this is one of the most constructive, and one of the most sensible, and also one of the most exciting programs that this Nation has ever undertaken. I don't say that just because the most ardent and most active and most enthusiastic supporter of this program happens to be the honorary national chairman, Mrs. Johnson.

We have taken up the age-old challenge of poverty and we don't intend to lose generations of our children to this enemy of the human race.

This program, like so many others, will succeed in proportion as it is supported by voluntary assistance and understanding from all of our people. So we are going to need a million good neighbors – volunteers – who will give their time for a few hours each week caring for these children, helping in a hundred ways to draw out their potentials. . . .

ON MEDICARE
July 30, 1965

In the presence of former President Harry S Truman, Johnson signed the Medicare Bill, which provided medical care for Americans 65 or older under Social Security. President Kennedy had promoted a Medicare Bill without success during his Administration.

The people of the United States love and voted for Harry Truman, not because he gave them hell – but because he gave them hope.

I believe today that all America shares my joy that he is present now when the hope that he offered becomes a reality for millions of our fellow citizens.

I am so proud that this has come to pass in the Johnson administration. But it was really Harry Truman of Missouri who planted the seeds of compassion and duty which have today flowered into care for the sick, and serenity for the fearful.

Many men can make many proposals. Many men can draft many laws. But few have the piercing and humane eye which can see beyond the words to the people that they touch. Few can see past the speeches and the political battles to the doctor over there that is tending the infirm, and to the hospital that is receiving those in anguish, or feel in their heart painful wrath at the injustice which denies the miracle of healing to the old and to the poor. And fewer still have the courage to stake reputation, and position, and the effort of a lifetime upon such a cause when there are so few that share it. . . .

It was a generation ago that Harry Truman said, and I quote him: "Millions of our citizens do not now have a full measure of opportunity to achieve and to enjoy good health. Millions do not now have protection or security against the economic effects of sickness. And the time has now arrived for action to help them attain that opportunity and to help them get that protection."

Well, today, Mr. President, and my fellow Americans, we are taking such action—20 years later. . . . Because the need for this action is plain; and it is so clear indeed that we marvel not simply at the passage of this bill, but what we marvel at is that it took so many years to pass it. . . .

There are more than 18 million Americans over the age of 65. Most of them have low incomes. Most of them are threatened by illness and medical expenses that they cannot afford. . . . This insurance will help pay for care in hospitals, in skilled nursing homes, or in the home. And under a separate plan it will help meet the fees of the doctors.

Now here is how the plan will affect you.

During your working years, the people of America— you — will contribute through the social security program a small amount each payday for hospital insurance protection. For example, the average worker in 1966 will contribute about $1.50 per month. The employer will contribute a similar amount. And this will provide the funds to pay up to 90 days of hospital care for each illness, plus diagnostic care, and up to 100 home health visits after you are 65. And beginning in 1967, you will also be covered for up to 100 days of care in a skilled nursing home after a period of hospital care.

And under a separate plan, when you are 65 — that the Congress originated itself, in its own good judgment — you may be covered for medical and surgical fees whether you are in or out of the hospital. You will pay $3 per month after you are 65 and your Government will conribute an equal amount.

The benefits under the law are as varied and broad as the marvelous modern medicine itself. If it has a few defects – such as the method of payment of certain specialists – then I am confident those can be quickly remedied and I hope they will be.

No longer will older Americans be denied the healing miracle of modern medicine. No longer will illness crush and destroy the savings that they have so carefully put away over a lifetime so that they might enjoy dignity in their later years. No longer will young families see their own incomes, and their own hopes, eaten away simply because they are carrying out their deep moral obligations to their parents, and to their uncles, and their aunts.

And no longer will this Nation refuse the hand of justice to those who have given a lifetime of service and wisdom and labor to the progress of this progressive country. . . .

ON THE VOTING RIGHTS BILL
August 6, 1965

This civil rights bill was adopted to insure Negro voting rights by elimination of the use of literacy tests and other restrictive registration devices. It also permitted the use of Federal examiners to register Negroes where the registration process was impeded.

Today is a triumph for freedom as huge as any victory that has ever been won on any battlefield. Yet to seize the meaning of this day, we must recall darker times.

Three and a half centuries ago the first Negroes arrived at Jamestown. They did not arrive in brave ships in search of a home for freedom. They did not mingle fear and joy, in expectation that in this New World anything would be possible to a man strong enough to reach for it. They came in darkness and they came in chains.

And today we strike away the last major shackle of those fierce and ancient bonds. Today the Negro story and the American story fuse and blend. . . .

When pioneers subdued a continent to the need of man, they did not tame it for the Negro. When the Liberty Bell rang out in Philadelphia, it did not toll for the Negro. When Andrew Jackson threw open the doors of democracy, they did not open for the Negro.

It was only at Appomattox, a century ago, that an American victory was also a Negro victory. And the two rivers — one shining with promise, the other dark-stained with oppression — began to move toward one another.

Yet, for almost a century the promise of that day was not fulfilled. Today is a towering and certain mark that, in this generation, that promise will be kept. In our time the two currents will finally mingle and rush as one great stream across the uncertain and the marvelous years of the America that is yet to come.

This act flows from a clear and simple wrong. Its only purpose is to right that wrong. Millions of Americans are denied the right to vote because of their color. This law will ensure them the right to vote. The wrong is one which no American, in his heart, can justify. The right is one which no American, true to our principles, can deny. . . .

Last year I said, "Until every qualified person regardless of . . . the color of his skin has the right, unquestioned and unrestrained, to go in and cast his ballot in every precinct in this great land of ours, I am not going to be satisfied."

And then last March, with the outrage of Selma still fresh, I came down to this Capitol one evening and asked the Congress and the people for swift and for sweeping action to guarantee to every man and woman the right to vote. In less than 48 hours I sent the Voting Rights Act of 1965 to the Congress. In little more than 4 months the Congress, with overwhelming majorities, enacted one of the most monumental laws in the entire history of American freedom.

The Members of the Congress, and the many private citizens, who worked to shape and pass this bill will share a place of honor in our history for this one act alone.

There were those who said this is an old injustice, and there is no need to hurry. But 95 years have passed since the 15th amendment gave all Negroes the right to vote.

And the time for waiting is gone.

There were those who said smaller and more gradual measures should be tried. But they had been tried. For years and years they had been tried, and tried, and tried, and they had failed, and failed, and failed. And the time for failure is gone.

There were those who said that this is a many-sided and very complex problem. But however viewed, the denial of the right to vote is still a deadly wrong. And the time for injustice has gone.

This law covers many pages. But the heart of the act is plain. Wherever, by clear and objective standards, States and counties are using regulations, or laws, or tests to deny the right to vote, then they will be struck down. If it is clear that State officials still intend to discriminate, then Federal examiners will be sent in to register all eligible voters. When the prospect of discrimination is gone, the examiners will be immediately withdrawn.

And, under this act, if any county anywhere in this Nation does not want Federal intervention it need only open its polling places to all of its people. . . .

Today what is perhaps the last of the legal barriers is tumbling. There will be many actions and many difficulties before the rights woven into law are also woven into the fabric of our Nation. But the struggle for equality must now move toward a different battlefield.

It is nothing less than granting every American Negro his freedom to enter the mainstream of American life: not the conformity that blurs enriching differences of culture and tradition, but rather the opportunity that gives each a chance to choose. . . .

For it is not enough just to give men rights. They must be able to use those rights in their personal pursuit of happiness. The wounds and the weaknesses, the outward walls and the inward scars which diminish achievement are the work of American society. We must all now help to end them — help to end them through expanding programs already devised and through new ones to search out and forever end the special handicaps of those who are black in a Nation that happens to be mostly white. . . .

So, we will move step by step — often painfully but, I think, with clear vision — along the path toward American freedom. . . .

The central fact of American civilization — one so hard for others to understand — is that freedom and justice and the dignity of man are not just words to us. We believe in them. Under all the growth and the tumult and abundance, we believe. And so, as long as some among us are oppressed — and we are part of that oppression — it must blunt our faith and sap the strength of our high purpose.

Thus, this is a victory for the freedom of the American Negro. But it is also a victory for the freedom of the American Nation. And every family across this great, entire, searching land will live stronger in liberty, will live more splendid in expectation, and will be prouder to be American because of the act that you have passed that I will sign today.

ON THE IMMIGRATION ACT
October 3, 1965

*President Johnson regarded the Immigration Act of 1965
as one of the most important pieces of legislation passed
during his Administrations. This revision of the 1924
National Origins Act aided the emigration of Cuban refugees who began fleeing Castro controlled Cuba in September, 1965*

. . . . This bill that we will sign today is not a revolutionary bill.
It does not affect the lives of millions. It will not reshape the struc-
ture of our daily lives, or really add importantly to either our wealth
or our power. Yet it is still one of the most important acts of this
administration. For it does repair a very deep and painful flaw in the
fabric of American justice. It corrects a cruel and enduring wrong in
the conduct of the American Nation. . . .

I have come here to thank personally each Member of the Congress
who labored so long and so valiantly to make this occasion come true
today, and to make this bill a reality. I cannot mention all their names,
for it would take much too long, but my gratitude – and that of this
Nation – belongs to the 89th Congress. We are indebted, too, to the
vision of the late beloved President John Fitzgerald Kennedy, and to
the support given to this measure by the then Attorney General and
now Senator, Robert F. Kennedy. . . .

This bill says simply that from this day forth those wishing to im-
migrate to America shall be admitted on the basis of their skills and
their close relationship to those already here. This is a simple test,
and it is a fair test. Those who can contribute most to this country –
to its growth, to its strength, to its spirit – will be the first that are
admitted to this land.

The fairness of this standard is so selfevident that we may well
wonder that it has not always been applied. Yet the fact is that for over
four decades the immigration policy of the United States has been
twisted and has been distorted by the harsh injustice of the national
origins quota system.

Under that system the ability of new immigrants to come to America depended upon the country of their birth. Only 3 countries were
allowed to supply 70 percent of all the immigrants. Families were kept
apart because a husband or a wife or a child had been born in the wrong
place. Men of needed skill and talent were denied entrance because they
came from southern or eastern Europe or from one of the developing
countinents.

This system violated the basic principle of American democracy — the principle that values and rewards each man on the basis of his merit as a man.

It has been un-American in the highest sense, because it has been untrue to the faith that brought thousands to these shores even before we were a country.

Today, with my signature, this system is abolished. . . .

. . . . Miami will serve as a port of entry and a temporary stopping place for refugees as they settle in other parts of this country.

And to all the voluntary agencies in the United States, I appeal for their continuation and expansion of their magnificent work. Their help is needed in the reception and the settlement of those who choose to leave Cuba. The Federal Government will work closely with these agencies in their tasks of charity and brotherhood.

I want all the people of this great land of ours to know of the really enormous contribution which the compassionate citizens of Florida have made to humanity and to decency. And all States in this Union can join with Florida now in extending the hand of helpfulness and humanity to our Cuban brothers.

The lesson of our times is sharp and clear in this movement of people from one land to another. Once again, it stamps the mark of failure on a regime when many of its citizens voluntarily choose to leave the land of their birth for a more hopeful home in America. The future holds little hope for any government where the present holds no hope for the people.

And so we Americans will welcome these Cuban people. For the tides of history run strong, and in another day they can return to their homeland to find it cleansed of terror and free from fear.

Over my shoulders here you can see Ellis Island, whose vacant corridors echo today the joyous sound of long ago voices.

And today we can all believe that the lamp of this grand old lady is brighter today — and the golden door that she guards gleams more brilliantly in the light of an increased liberty for the people from all the countries of the globe.

Thank you very much.

STATE OF THE UNION ADDRESS
January 12, 1966

In a very long Annual Message to Congress and the nation, Johnson again stated his goals for the "Great Society," but the larger part of the speech was given over to foreign policy, especially the war in Vietnam.

I come before you tonight to report on the State of the Union for the third time. . . .

Our Nation tonight is engaged in a brutal and bitter conflict in Vietnam. Later on I want to discuss that struggle in some detail with you. It just must be the center of our concerns.

But we will not permit those who fire upon us in Vietnam to win a victory over the desires and the intentions of all the American people. This Nation is mighty enough, its society is healthy enough, its people are strong enough, to pursue our goals in the rest of the world while still building a Great Society here at home. And that is what I have come here to ask of you tonight.

I recommend that you provide the resources to carry forward, with full vigor, the great health and education programs that you enacted into law last year.

I recommend that we prosecute with vigor and determination our war on poverty.

I recommend that you give a new and daring direction to our foreign aid program, designed to make a maximum attack on hunger and disease and ignorance in those countries that are determined to help themselves, and to help those nations that are trying to control population growth.

I recommend that you make it possible to expand trade between the United States and Eastern Europe and the Soviet Union.

I recommend to you a program to rebuild completely, on a scale never before attempted, entire central and slum areas of several of our cities in America.

I recommend that you attack the wasteful and degrading poisoning of our rivers, and, as the cornerstone of this effort, clean completely entire large river basins.

I recommend that you meet the growing menace of crime in the streets by building up law enforcement and by revitalizing the entire Federal system from prevention to probation.

I recommend that you take additional steps to insure equal justice to all of our people by effectively enforcing nondiscrimination in Federal and State jury selection, by making it a serious Federal crime to obstruct public and private efforts to secure civil rights, and by outlawing discrimination in the sale and rental of housing.

I recommend that you help me modernize and streamline the Federal Government by creating a new Cabinet level Department of Transportation and reorganizing several existing agencies. In turn, I will restructure our civil service in the top grades so that men and women can easily be assigned to jobs where they are most needed, and ability will be both required as well as rewarded.

I will ask you to make it possible for Members of the House of Representatives to work more effectively in the service of the Nation through a constitutional amendment extending the term of a Congressman to 4 years, concurrent with that of the President.

Because of Vietnam we cannot do all that we should, or all that we would like to do.

We will ruthlessly attack waste and inefficiency. We will make sure that every dollar is spent with the thrift and with the commonsense which recognizes how hard the taxpayer worked in order to earn it.

We will continue to meet the needs of our people by continuing to develop the Great Society. . . .

Tonight the cup of peril is full in Vietnam.

That conflict is not an isolated episode, but another great event in the policy that we have followed with strong consistency since World War II.

The touchstone of that policy is the interest of the United States — the welfare and the freedom of the people of the United States. But nations sink when they see that interest only through a narrow glass. In a world that has grown small and dangerous, pursuit of narrow aims could bring decay and even disaster.

An America that is mighty beyond description — yet living in a hostile or despairing world — would be neither safe nor free to build a civilization to liberate the spirit of man. In this pursuit we helped rebuild Western Europe. We gave our aid to Greece and Turkey, and we defended the freedom of Berlin.

In this pursuit we have helped new nations toward independence. We have extended the helping hand of the Peace Corps and carried forward the largest program of economic assistance in the world. And in this pursuit we work to build a hemisphere of democracy and of social justice.

In this pursuit we have defended against Communist aggression — in Korea under President Truman — in the Formosa Straits under President Eisenhower — in Cuba under President Kennedy — and again in Vietnam.

Tonight Vietnam must hold the center of our attention, but across the world problems and opportunities crowd in on the American Nation. I will discuss them fully in the months to come, and I will follow the five continuing lines of policy that America has followed under its last four Presidents.

(1) The first principle is strength.

Tonight I can tell you that we are strong enough to keep all of our commitments. We will need expenditures of $58.3 billion for the next fiscal year to maintain this necessary defense might.

While special Vietnam expenditures for the next fiscal year are estimated to increase by $5.8 billion, I can tell you that all the other expenditures put together in the entire Federal budget will rise this coming year by only $.6 billion. This is true because of the stringent cost-conscious economy program inaugurated in the Defense Department, and followed by the other departments of Government.

(2) A second principle of policy is the effort to control, and to reduce, and to ultimately eliminate the modern engines of destruction.

We will vigorously pursue existing proposals – and seek new ones – to control arms and to stop the spread of nuclear weapons.

(3) A third major principle of our foreign policy is to help build those associations of nations which reflect the opportunities and the necessities of the modern world.

By strengthening the common defense, by stimulating world commerce, by meeting new hopes, these associations serve the cause of a flourishing world.

We will take new steps this year to help strengthen the Alliance for Progress, the unity of Europe, the community of the Atlantic, the regional organizations of developing continents, and that supreme association – the United Nations.

We will work to strengthen economic cooperation, to reduce barriers to trade, and to improve international finance.

(4) A fourth enduring strand of policy has been to help improve the life of man.

From the Marshall plan to this very moment tonight, that policy has rested on the claims of compassion, and the certain knowledge that only a people advancing in expectation will build secure and peaceful lands.

This year I propose major new directions in our program of foreign assistance to help those countries who will help themselves.

We will conduct a worldwide attack on the problems of hunger and disease and ignorance.

We will place the matchless skill and the resources of our own great America, in farming and in fertilizers, at the service of those countries committed to develop a modern agriculture.

We will aid those who educate the young in other lands, and we will give children in other continents the same head start that we are trying to give our own children. To advance these ends I will propose the International Education Act of 1966.

I will also propose the International Health Act of 1966 to strike at disease by a new effort to bring modern skills and knowledge to the uncared-for, those suffering in the world, and by trying to wipe out smallpox and malaria and control yellow fever over most of the world during this next decade. . . .

Last year the nature of the war in Vietnam changed again. Swiftly increasing numbers of armed men from the North crossed the borders to join forces that were already in the South. Attack and terror increased, spurred and encouraged by the belief that the United States lacked the will to continue and that their victory was near.

Despite our desire to limit conflict, it was necessary to act: to hold back the mounting aggression, to give courage to the people of the South, and to make our firmness clear to the North. Thus we began limited air action against military targets in North Vietnam. We increased our fighting force to its present strength tonight of 190,000 men.

These moves have not ended the aggression but they have prevented its success. The aims of the enemy have been put out of reach by the skill and the bravery of Americans and their allies — and by the enduring courage of the South Vietnamese who, I can tell you, have lost eight men last year for every one of ours.

The enemy is no longer close to victory. Time is no longer on his side. There is no cause to doubt the American commitment.

Our decision to stand firm has been matched by our desire for peace. In 1965 alone we had 300 private talks for peace in Vietnam, with friends and adversaries throughout the world.

In public statements and in private communications, to adversaries and to friends, in Rome and Warsaw, in Paris and Tokyo, in Africa and throughout this hemisphere, America has made her position abundantly clear.

We seek neither territory nor bases, economic domination or military alliance in Vietnam. We fight for the principle of self-determination — that the people of South Vietnam should be able to choose their own course, choose it in free elections without violence, without terror, and without fear.

The people of all Vietnam should make a free decision on the great question of reunification. . . .

But we will give our fighting men what they must have: every gun, and every dollar, and every decision — whatever the cost or whatever the challenge.

And we will continue to help the people of South Vietnam care for those that are ravaged by battle, create progress in the villages, and carry forward the healing hopes of peace as best they can amidst the uncertain terrors of war.

And let me be absolutely clear: The days may become months, and the months may become years, but we will stay as long as aggression commands us to battle.

There may be some who do not want peace, whose ambitions stretch so far that war in Vietnam is but a welcome and convenient episode in an immense design to subdue history to their will. But for others it must now be clear — the choice is not between peace and victory, it lies between peace and the ravages of a conflict from which they can only lose.

The people of Vietnam, North and South, seek the same things: the shared needs of man, the needs for food and shelter and education — the chance to build and work and till the soil, free from the arbitrary horrors of battle — the desire to walk in the dignity of those who master their own destiny. For many painful years, in war and revolution and infrequent peace, they have struggled to fulfill those needs.

It is a crime against mankind that so much courage, and so much will, and so many dreams, must be flung on the fires of war and death.

To all of those caught up in this conflict we therefore say again tonight: Let us choose peace, and with it the wondrous works of peace, and beyond that, the time when hope reaches toward consummation, and life is the servant of life.

In this work, we plan to discharge our duty to the people whom we serve. . . .

ON THE DEPARTMENT OF TRANSPORTATION
October 15, 1966

Recognizing the mammoth need for a Cabinet-Level De-
partment to handle the ever-growing transportation problem
in the United States, Johnson happily signed the bill cre-
ating this new Cabinet Department. Allan Boyd became
its first Secretary.

. . . . We have come to this historic East Room of the White House today to establish and to bring into being a Department of Transportation, the second Cabinet office to be added to the President's Cabinet in recent months.

This Department of Transportation that we are establishing will have a mammoth task — to untangle, to coordinate, and to build the national transportation system for America that America is deserving of. . . .

Among the many duties the new department will have, several deserve very special notice.

- To improve the safety in every means of transportation, safety of transportation, safety of our automobiles, our trains, our planes, and our ships.

- To bring new technology to every mode of transportation by supporting and promoting research and development.

- To solve our most pressing transportation problems.

In a few respects, this bill falls short of our original hopes. It does not include the Maritime Administration. As experience is gained in the department, I would hope that the Congress could reexamine its decision to leave this key transportation activity alone, outside its jurisdiction. . . .

Today you bring 31 agencies and their bureaus, going in all directions, into a single Department of Transportation under the guidance and leadership of a Secretary of Transportation.

I think in fairness, candor requires me to review that this recommendation was made many years ago by the Hoover Commission, headed by the distinguished former President. This recommendation was urged upon the Congress and the people, and recommended many years ago by a most distinguished and popular President, President Dwight David Eisenhower.

This recommendation was made and urged upon the President and the Congress many years ago by the Senate Commerce Committee, and by dozens and dozens of enlightened, intelligent Members of both House of both parties. . . . and we salute everyone who contributed to finally bringing our performance in line with our promise.

STATE OF THE UNION ADDRESS
January 11, 1967

*In a rather short, dull message, Johnson talked in terms
of past accomplishments, and repeated his determination
to bring the war in Vietnam to a successful conclusion.*

. . . . I have come here tonight to report to you that this is a time
of testing for our Nation.

At home, the question is whether we will continue working for
better opportunities for all Americans, when most Americans are already living better than any people in history.

Abroad, the question is whether we have the staying power to fight
a very costly war, when the objective is limited and the danger to us is
seemingly remote.

So our test is not whether we shrink from our country's cause when
the dangers to us are obvious and close at hand, but, rather, whether
we carry on when they seem obscure and distant — and some think
that it is safe to lay down our burdens.

I have come tonight to ask this Congress and this Nation to resolve
that issue: to meet our commitments at home and abroad — to continue
to build a better America — and to reaffirm this Nation's allegiance
to freedom. . . .

I come now finally to Southeast Asia — and to Vietnam in particular.
Soon I will submit to the Congress a detailed report on that situation.
Tonight I want to just review the essential points as briefly as I can.

We are in Vietnam because the United States of America and our
allies are committed by the SEATO Treaty to "act to meet the common danger" of aggression in Southeast Asia.

We are in Vietnam because an international agreement signed by the
United States, North Vietnam, and others in 1962 is being systematical-
ly violated by the Communists. That violation threatens the independence of all the small nations in Southeast Asia, and threatens the
peace of the entire region and perhaps the world.

We are there because the people of South Vietnam have as much
right to remain non-Communist — if that is what they choose — as
North Vietnam has to remain Communist.

We are there because the Congress has pledged by solemn vote to
take all necessary measures to prevent further aggression. . . .

We have chosen to fight a limited war in Vietnam in an attempt to
prevent a larger war — a war almost certain to follow, I believe, if
the Communists succeed in overrunning and taking over South Vietnam

by aggression and by force. I believe, and I am supported by some authority, that if they are not checked now the world can expect to pay a greater price to check them later.

That is what our statesmen said when they debated this treaty, and that is why it was ratified 82 to 1 by the Senate many years ago. . . .

I think I reveal no secret when I tell you that we are dealing with a stubborn adversary who is committed to the use of force and terror to settle political questions.

I wish I could report to you that the conflict is almost over. This I cannot do. We face more cost, more loss, and more agony. For the end is not yet. I cannot promise you that it will come this year – or come next year. Our adversary still believes, I think, tonight, that he can go on fighting longer than we can, and longer than we and our allies will be prepared to stand up and resist.

Our men in that area – there are nearly 500,000 now – have borne well "the burden and the heat of the day." Their efforts have deprived the Communist enemy of the victory that he sought and that he expected a year ago. We have steadily frustrated his main forces. General Westmoreland reports that the enemy can no longer succeed on the battlefield.

So I must say to you that our pressure must be sustained – and will be sustained – until he realizes that the war he started is costing him more than he can ever gain. . . .

How long it will take I cannot prophesy. I only know that the will of the American people, I think, is tonight being tested.

Whether we can fight a war of limited objectives over a period of time, and keep alive the hope of independence and stability for people other than ourselves; whether we can continue to act with restraint when the temptation to "get it over with" is inviting but dangerous; whether we can accept the necessity of choosing "a great evil in order to ward off a greater"; whether we can do these without arousing the hatreds and the passions that are ordinarily loosed in time of war – on all these questions so much turns. . . .

For all the disorders that we must deal with, and all the frustrations that concern us, and all the anxieties that we are called upon to resolve, for all the issues we must face with the agony that attends them, let us remember that "those who expect to reap the blessings of freedom must, like men, undergo the fatigues of supporting it." . . .

So with your understanding, I would hope your confidence, and your support, we are going to persist – and we are going to succeed.

ON THE GLASSBORO SUMMIT MEETING
June 25, 1967

When Premier Aleksei Kosygin came to the United States to attend the General Assembly of the United Nations, a hurried summit meeting between Johnson and the Premier was arranged. The talks were far ranging, but dealt primarily with the Vietnam War. The first selection comes from remarks made to the crowd in Glassboro, New Jersey, and the second was the President's comments on his return to the White House.

On my return tonight to the White House after 2 days of talks at Hollybush, I want to make this brief report to the American people.

We continued our discussions today in the same spirit in which we began them on Friday — a spirit of direct, face-to-face exchanges between leaders with very heavy responsibilities.

You will not be surprised to know that these two meetings have not solved all of our problems. On some we have made progress — great progress in reducing misunderstanding, I think, and in reaffirming our common commitment to seek agreement.

I think we made that kind of progress, for example, on the question of arms limitation. We have agreed this afternoon that Secretary of State Rusk and Mr. Gromyko will pursue this subject further in New York in the days ahead.

I must report that no agreement is readily in sight on the Middle Eastern crisis, and that our well known differences over Vietnam continue. . . .

When nations have deeply different positions, as we do on these issues, they do not come to agreement merely by improving their understanding of each other's views. But such improvement helps. Sometimes in such discussions you can find elements — beginnings — hopeful fractions of common ground even within a general disagreement. It was so in the Middle East 2 weeks ago when we agreed on the need for a prompt cease-fire. And it is so today in respect to such simple propositions as that every state has a right to live; that there should be an end to the war in the Middle East; and that in the right circumstances there should be withdrawal of troops.

This is a long way from agreement, but it is a long way, also, from total difference.

On Vietnam, the area of agreement is smaller. It is defined by the fact that the dangers and the difficulties of any one area must never be allowed to become a cause of wider conflict. Yet even in Vietnam

I was able to make it very clear, with no third party between us, that we will match and we will outmatch every step to peace that others may be ready to take.

As I warned on Friday, and as I just must warn again on this Sunday afternoon another thing that I said on last Friday: that it does help a lot to sit down and look at a man right in the eye and try to reason with him, particularly if he is trying to reason with you.

We may have differences and difficulties ahead, but I think they will be lessened and not increased by our new knowledge of each other. . . .

ON ESTABLISHING THE PRESIDENT'S COMMISSION ON CIVIL DISORDERS
July 27, 1967

During the summer of 1967, a number of Negro riots rocked the nation. Hardly a major city in the country escaped the urban riots, Johnson appointed a special advisory commission on Civil Disorders.

My fellow Americans:

We have endured a week such as no nation should live through: a time of violence and tragedy.

For a few minutes tonight, I want to talk about that tragedy — and I want to talk about the deeper questions it raises for us all.

I am tonight appointing a special Advisory Commission on Civil Disorders.

Governor Otto Kerner of Illinois has agreed to serve as Chairman. Mayor John Lindsay of New York will serve as Vice Chairman. Its other members will include Fred R. Harris, Senator from Oklahoma; Edward W. Brooke, United States Senator from Massachusetts; James C. Corman, U.S. Representative from California, 22nd District, Los Angeles; William M. McCulloch, the U.S. Representative from the State of Ohio, the 4th District; I.W. Abel, the president of the United Steel Workers; Charles B. Thornton, the president, director, and chairman of the board of Litton Industries, Inc.; Roy Wilkins, the executive director of the NAACP; Katherine Graham Peden, the Commissioner of Commerce of the State of Kentucky; Herbert Jenkins, the chief of police, Atlanta, Georgia.

The Commission will investigate the origins of the recent disorders in our cities. It will make recommendations — to me, to the Congress, to the State Governors, and to the mayors — for measures to prevent or contain such disasters in the future.

In their work, the Commission members will have access to the facts that are gathered by Director Edgar Hoover and the Federal Bureau of Investigation. The FBI will continue to exercise its full authority to investigate these riots, in accordance with my standing instructions, and continue to search for evidence of conspiracy.

But even before the Commission begins its work, and even before all the evidence is in, there are some things that we can tell about the outbreaks of this summer.

First — let there be no mistake about it — the looting, arson, plunder, and pillage which have occurred are not part of the civil rights protest. There is no American right to loot stores, or to burn buildings, or to fire rifles from the rooftops. That is crime — and crime must be dealt with forcefully, and swiftly, and certainly — under law.

Innocent people, Negro and white, have been killed. Damage to property — owned by Negroes and whites — is calamitous. Worst of all, fear and bitterness which have been loosed will take long months to erase.

The criminals who committed these acts of violence against the people deserve to be punished — and they must be punished. Explanations may be offered, but nothing can excuse what they have done.

There will be attempts to interpret the events of the past few days. But when violence strikes, then those in public responsibility have an immediate and a very different job: not to analyze, but to end disorder.

I have directed the Secretary of Defense to issue new training standards for riot control procedures immediately to National Guard units across the country. Through the Continental Army Command, this expanded training will begin immediately. The National Guard must have the ability to respond effectively, quickly, and appropriately, in conditions of disorder and violence.

Those charged with the responsibility of law enforcement should, and must, be respected by all of our people. The violence must be stopped, quickly, finally, and permanently.

Not even the sternest police action, nor the most effective Federal troops, can ever create lasting peace in our cities.

The only genuine, long-range solution for what has happened lies in an attack — mounted at every level — upon the conditions that breed despair and violence. All of us know what those conditions are: ignorance, discrimination, slums, poverty, disease, not enough jobs. We should attack these conditions — not because we are frightened by conflict, but because we are fired by conscience. We should attack them because there is simply no other way to achieve a decent and orderly society in America. . . .

So, my fellow citizens, let us go about our work. Let us clear the streets of rubble and quench the fires that hatred set. Let us feed and care for those who have suffered at the rioters' hands — but let there be no bonus or reward or salutes for those who have inflicted that suffering.

Let us resolve that this violence is going to stop and there will be no bonus to flow from it. We can stop it. We must stop it. We will stop it. . . .

ON THE NUCLEAR NON-PROLIFERATION TREATY
August 24, 1967

Following the Kennedy Administration's successful achievement of the Limited Nuclear Test Ban Treaty in 1963, Johnson proposed additional safeguards to bring about a nuclear detente with the Soviet Union. The Non-Proliferation Treaty was one such attempt, and was later signed by the United States and the Soviet Union in 1968.

Today at Geneva the United States and the Soviet Union as Co-chairmen of the Eighteen-Nation Disarmament Committee are submitting to the Committee a draft treaty to stop the spread of nuclear weapons.

For more than 20 years, the world has watched with growing fear as nuclear weapons have spread.

Since 1945, five nations have come into possession of these dreadful weapons. We believe now — as we did then — that even one such nation is too many. But the issue now is not whether some have nuclear weapons while others do not. The issue is whether the nations will agree to prevent a bad situation from becoming worse.

Today, for the first time, we have within our reach an instrument which permits us to make a choice.

The submission of a draft treaty brings us to the final and most critical stage of this effort. The draft will be available for consideration by all governments, and for negotiation by the Conference.

The treaty must reconcile the interests of nations with our interest as a community of human beings on a small planet. The treaty must be responsive to the needs and problems of all the nations of the world — great and small, aligned and nonaligned, nuclear and nonnuclear.

It must add to the security of all.

It must encourage the development and use of nuclear energy for peaceful purposes.

It must provide adequate protection against the corruption of the peaceful atom to its use for weapons of war.

I am convinced that we are today offering an instrument that will meet these requirements. . . .

The Eighteen-Nation Committee on Disarmament now has before it the opportunity to make a cardinal contribution to man's safety and peace.

STATE OF THE UNION ADDRESS
January 17, 1968

*In this annual message, Johnson reiterated his desire
for peace in Vietnam, but continued to stick to his hard-
line, get tough approach. A large number of Senators and
Congressmen did not attend this annual joint-session.*

. . . . I report to you that our country is challenged at home and
abroad:

— That it is our will that is being tried, and not our strength: our
sense of purpose, and not our ability to achieve a better America;

— That we have the strength to meet our every challenge, the
physical strength to hold the course of decency and compassion at
home; and the moral strength to support the cause of peace in the
world.

And I report to you that I believe, with abiding conviction, that this
people — nurtured by their deep faith, tutored by their hard lessons,
moved by their high aspirations — have the will to meet the trials that
these times impose. . . .

I have just recently returned from a very fruitful visit and talks
with His Holiness the Pope, and I share his hope, as he expressed it
earler today, that both sides will extend themselves in an effort to
bring an end to the war in Vietnam, and I have today assured him that
we and our allies will do our full part to bring this about.

Since I spoke to you last January other events have occurred that
have major consequences for world peace.

KENNEDY ROUND PRAISED

The Kennedy Round achieved the greatest reduction in tariff barriers in all the history of trade negotiations.

The nations of Latin America at Punta del Este resolved to move
toward economic integration.

In Asia, the nations from Korea and Japan to Indonesia and Singa-
pore worked behind America's shield to strengthen their economics
and to broaden their political cooperation.

And (in) Africa, from which the distinguished Vice President has
just returned, he reports to me that there is a spirit of regional cooperation that is beginning to take hold in very practical ways.

And these events we all welcome. And yet, since I last reported to
you, we and the world have been confronted by a number of crises.

During the Arab-Israeli war last June, the hot line between Washington and Moscow was used for the first time in our history. A ceasefire was achieved without a major power confrontation.

Now the nations of the Middle East have the opportunity to cooperate with Ambassador Jarring's U.N. mission — and they have the responsibility to find the terms of living together in stable peace and dignity, and we shall do all in our power to help them achieve that result.

Not far from this scene of conflict, a crisis flared on Cyprus, involving two peoples who are America's friends — Greece and Turkey. Our very able representative, Mr. Cyrus Vance, and others helped to ease this tension.

Turmoil continues on the mainland of China after a year of violent disruption. The radical extremism of their government has isolated the Chinese people behind their own borders. The United States, however, remains willing to permit the travel of journalists to both of our countries; to undertake cultural and educational exchanges; and to talk about the exchange of basic food crop materials.

Since I spoke to you last the United States and the Soviet Union have taken several important steps toward the goal of international cooperation. . . .

Because we believe that the nuclear danger must be narrowed, we have worked with the Soviet Union and with other nations to reach an agreement that will halt the spread of nuclear weapons. . . .

We achieved in 1967 a consular treaty with the Soviets; the first commercial air agreement between the two countries and a treaty banning weapons in outer space. We shall sign and submit to the Senate shortly a new treaty with the Soviets and with others for the protection of astronauts.

Serious differences still remain between us, yet in these relations we have made some progress since Vienna and the Berlin Wall and the Cuban missile crisis. . . .

Now let me speak about some matters here at home.

Tonight our nation is accomplishing more for its people than has ever been accomplished before. Americans are prosperous as men have never been in recorded history.

Yet, there is in the land a certain restlessness, a questioning.

The total of our nation's annual production is now above $800-billion. For 83 months this nation has been on a steady, upward trend of growth. All about them, most American families can see the evidence of growing abundance.

Higher paychecks; humming factories; new cars moving down new highways; more and more families own their own homes equipped with more than 70 million television sets; a new college is founded every year. Today more than half of the high school graduates go on to college.

And there are hundreds of thousands of fathers and mothers who never completed grammar school — who will see their children graduate from college. . . .

And while we have accomplished much, much remains for us to meet, and much remains for us to master.

— In some areas, the jobless rate is still three or four times the national average.

— Violence has shown its face in some of our cities.

— Crime increases on our streets.

— Income for farm workers remains far behind that for urban workers; and parity for our farmers, who produce our food, is still just a hope — and not an achievement.

— New housing construction is far less than we need – to assure decent shelters for every family.

— Hospital and medical costs are high, and they are rising.

— Many rivers — and the air in many cities — remain badly polluted.

And our citizens suffer from breathing that air.

We lived with conditions like these for many, many years. But much that we once accepted as inevitable, we now find absolutely intolerable.

In our cities last summer, we saw how wide is the gulf for some Americans between the promise and the reality of our society.

And we know that we cannot change all of this in a day. It represents the bitter consequences of more than three centuries.

But the issue is not whether we can change this; the issue is whether we will change this.

Well, I know we can. and I believe we will.

This then is the work that we should do in the months that are ahead of us here in this Congress. . . .

ON THE SEIZURE OF THE U. S. S. PUEBLO
January 26, 1968

On January 23, North Korean patrol boats boarded and seized a United States surveillance ship, the U.S.S. Pueblo, in international waters, and took the crew prisoner. It was not until December that the Pueblo's *crew was released.*

Over the past 15 months the North Koreans have pursued a stepped-up campaign of violence against South Korea and the American troops in the area of the demilitarized zone. Armed raider teams in very large numbers have been sent into South Korea to engage in sabotage and assassination.

On Jan. 19, a 31-man team of North Korean raiders invaded Seoul with the object of murdering the President of the Republic of Korea. In many of these aggressive actions Korean and American soldiers have been killed and wounded.

The North Koreans are apparently attempting to intimidate the South Koreans and are trying to interrupt the growing spirit of confidence and progress in the Republic of Korea. These attacks may also be an attempt by the Communists to divert South Korean and United States military resources, which together are now successfully resisting aggression in Vietnam.

This week the North Koreans committed yet another wanton and aggressive act by seizing an American ship and its crew in international waters. Clearly this cannot be accepted.

We are doing two things: first, we are very shortly today taking the question before the Security Council of the United Nations. The best result would be for the whole world community to persuade North Korea to return our ship and our men and to stop the dangerous course of aggression against South Korea.

We have been making other diplomatic efforts as well. We shall continue to use every means available to find a prompt and a peaceful solution to the problem.

Second, we have taken and we are taking certain precautionary measures to make sure that our military forces are preapred for any contingency that might arise in this area.

These actions do not involve in any way a reduction of our forces in Vietnam.

I hope that the North Koreans will recognize the gravity of the situation which they have created. I am confident that the American people will exhibit in this crisis, as they have in other crises, determination and unity.

ON THE BOMBING HALT OF NORTH VIETNAM, ON HIS DECISION NOT TO SEEK REELECTION
March 31, 1968

In this televised speech to the nation, Johnson announced his decision to stop bombing ninety percent of North Vietnam and dramatically stated that he would not be a candidate for reelection.

Tonight I want to speak to you of peace in Vietnam and Southeast Asia.

No other question so preoccupies our people. No other dream so absorbs the 250 million human beings who live in that part of the world. No other goal motivates American policy in Southeast Asia. . . .

There is no need to delay the talks that could bring an end to this long and this bloody war.

Tonight, I renew the offer I made last August: to stop the bombardment of North Vietnam. We ask that talks begin promptly, that they be serious talks on the substance of peace. We assume that during those talks Hanoi will not take advantage of our restraint.

We are prepared to move immediately toward peace through negotiations. So tonight, in the hope that this action will lead to early talks, I am taking the first step to de-escalate the conflict. We are reducing — substantially reducing — the present level of hostilities, and we are doing so unilaterally and at once.

Tonight I have ordered our aircraft and our naval vessels to make no attacks on North Vietnam except in the area north of the demilitarized zone where the continuing enemy build-up directly threatens allied forward positions and where the movement of their troops and supplies are clearly related to that threat.

The area in which we are stopping our attacks includes almost 90 percent of North Vietnam's population, and most of its territory. Thus there will be no attacks around the principal populated areas, or in the food-producing areas of North Vietnam.

Now as in the past, the United States is ready to send its representatives to any forum, at any time, to discuss the means of bringing this ugly war to an end.

I am designating one of our most distinguished Americans, Ambassador Averell Harriman, as my personal representative for such talks. In addition, I have asked Ambassador Llewellyn Thompson, who returned from Moscow for consultation, to be available to join Ambassador Harriman at Geneva or any other suitable place — just as soon as Hanoi agrees to a conference.

I call upon President Ho Chi Minh to respond positively, and favorably, to this new step toward peace.

But if peace does not come now through negotiations, it will come when Hanoi understands that our common resolve is unshakable, and our common strength is invincible. . . .

Finally, my fellow Americans, let me say this:

Of those to whom much is given much is asked. I cannot say — and no man could say — that no more will be asked of us. Yet I believe that now, no less than when the decade began, this generation of Americans is willing to pay the price, bear any burden, meet any hardship, support any friend, oppose any foe, to assure the survival, and the success, of liberty.

Since those words were spoken by John F. Kennedy, the people of America have kept that compact with mankind's noblest cause. And we shall continue to keep it.

ORDER OF LOYALTIES LISTED

This I believe very deeply. Throughout my entire public career I have followed the personal philosophy that I am a free man, an American, a public servant and a member of my party — in that order — always and only. . . .

There is division in the American house now. There is divisiveness among us all tonight. And holding the trust that is mine, as President of all the people, I cannot disregard the peril of the progress of the American people and the hope and the prospect of peace for all peoples, so I would ask all Americans whatever their personal interest or concern to guard against divisiveness and all of its ugly consequences.

Fifty-two months and ten days ago, in a moment of tragedy and trauma, the duties of this office fell upon me.

I asked then for your help, and God's, that we might continue America on its course binding up our wounds, healing our history, moving forward in new unity to clear the American agenda and to keep the American commitment for all of our people.

United we have kept that commitment. And united we have enlarged that commitment. And through all time to come I think America will be a stronger nation, a more just society, a land of greater opportunity and fulfillment because of what we have all done together in these years of unparalleled achievement.

Our reward will come in the life of freedom and peace and hope that our children will enjoy through ages ahead.

What we won when all of our people united just must not now be lost in suspicion and distrust and selfishness and politics among any of our people. And believing this as I do I have concluded that I should not permit the Presidency to become involved in the partisan divisions that are developing in this political year.

With American sons in the fields far away, with America's future under challenge right here at home, with our hopes and the world's hopes for peace in the balance every day, I do not believe that I should devote an hour or a day of my time to any personal partisan causes or to any duties other than the awesome duties of this office — the Presidency of your country.

Accordinging, I shall not seek, and I will not accept, the nomination of my party for another term as your President. But let men everywhere know, however, that a strong and a confident and a vigilant America stands ready tonight to seek an honorable peace; and stands ready tonight to defend an honored cause, whatever the price, whatever the burden, whatever the sacrifice that duty may require.

Thank you for listening. Good night, and God bless all of you.

ON VIOLENCE IN AMERICA
June 5, 1968

The shooting of Robert F. Kennedy on June 5, prompted Johnson, in a nationally televised speech, to name a Commission on Violence to examine this phenomenon of American life. The short message was also a tribute to the young Senator, who died the next day.

My fellow citizens, I speak to you this evening not only as your President, but as a fellow American that's shocked and dismayed as you are by the attempt on Senator Kennedy's life, deeply disturbed, as I know you are, by lawlessness and violence in our country, of which this tragedy is the latest spectacular example.

We do not know the reasons that inspired the attack on Senator Kennedy. We know only that a brilliant career of public service has been brutally interrupted, that a young leader of uncommon energy and dedication who has served his country tirelessly and well and whose voice and example has touched millions throughout the entire world has been senselessly and horribly stricken.

At this moment the outcome is still in the balance. We pray to God that he will spare Robert Kennedy and will restore him to full health and vigor. We pray this for the nation's sake, for the sake of his wife and his children, his father and his mother, and in memory of his brother, our beloved late President. . . .

Tonight this nation faces once again the consequences of lawlessness, hatred and unreason in its midst. It would be wrong, it would be self-deceptive, to ignore the connection between lawlessness and hatred and this act of violence.

It would be just as wrong and just as self-deceptive to conclude from this act that our country itself is sick, that it's lost its balance, that it's lost its sense of direction, even its common decency.

Two hundred million Americans did not strike down Robert Kennedy last night, any more than they struck down President John F. Kennedy in 1963, or Dr. Martin Luther King in April of this year.

But those awful events give us ample warning that in a climate of extremism, of disrespect for law, of contempt for the rights of others, violence may bring down the very best among us. And a nation that tolerates violence in any form cannot expect to be able to confine it to just minor outbursts.

My fellow citizens, we cannot, we just must not, tolerate the sway of violent men among us. We must not permit men that are filled with hatred and carelessness — and careless of innocent lives to dominate our streets and fill our homes with fear.

We cannot sanction the appeal to violence — no matter what its cause, no matter what the grievance from which it springs. . . .

A great nation can guarantee freedom for its people and the hope of progressive change only under the rule of law. . . .

Let the Congress pass laws to bring the insane traffic in guns to a halt as I have appealed to them time and time again to do. That will not in itself end the violence, but reason and experience tell us that it will slow it down, that it will spare many innocent lives.

Let us purge the hostility from our hearts, and let us practice moderation with our tongues.

Let us begin in the aftermath of this great tragedy to find a way to reverance life, to protect it, to extend its promise to all of our people, this nation and the people who have suffered griveously from violence and assassination.

For this reason I am appointing with the recommendation of the leadership of the Congress with whom I have talked this evening — a commission of most distinguished Americans to immediately examine this tragic phenomenon.

COMMISSION NAMED

They are Dr. Milton Eisenhower, the former distinguished president of Johns Hopkins University; Archbishop Terence Cooke of New York; Albert Jenner of Illinois; Ambassador Patrick Harris; Mr. Eric Hoffer; Senator Philip Hart Senator Roman Hruska; Congressman Hale Boggs; Congressman William McCullough and Judge Leon Higginbotham.

The commission will look into the causes, the occurence and the control of physical violence across this nation, from assassination that is motivated by prejudice and by ideology, and by politics and by insanity; to violence in our city streets and even in our homes.

What in the nature of our people and the environment of our society makes possible such murder and such violence?

How does it happen? What can be done to prevent assassination? What can be done to further protect public figures? What can be done to eliminate the basic causes of these aberrations?

Supported by the suggestions and recommendations of criminologists, sociologists and psychologists, all of our nation's medical and social sciences, we hope to learn why we inflict such suffering on ourselves.

And I hope and pray that we can learn how to stop it.

This is a sober time for our great democracy, but we are a strong and we are a resilient people who can, I hope, learn from our misfortunes, who can heal our wounds, who can build and find progress in public order.

We can. We must. So I appeal to every American citizen tonight — let us being tonight.

ON STRONG GUN CONTROL LAWS
June 6, 1968

President Johnson had been urging Congress to enact strong firearms control legislation since 1965. With the tragic death of Robert F. Kennedy, he renewed his endorsement of such legislation in a short special message to the Congress.

Today the nation cries out to the conscience of the Congress. Criminal violence from the muzzle of a gun has once again brought heartbreak to America. Surely this must be clear beyond question: The hour has come for the Congress to enact a strong and effective gun control law governing the full range of lethal weapons.

I have sought and I have fought for such a law through all the days of my Presidency. On many occasions before, I have spoken of the terrible toll inflicted on our people by firearms — 750,000 Americans dead since the turn of the century.

This is far more than have died at the hands of all of our enemies in all of the wars that we have fought — sorrow and suffering that just cannot be counted and fear that can never be measured.

Each year in this country, guns are involved in more than 6,500 murders. This compares with 30 in England, 99 in Canada, 68 in West Germany and 37 in Japan.

Forty-four thousand aggravated assaults are committed with guns in America each year. Fifty thousand robberies are committed with guns in America each year. Fifty thousand robberies are committed with guns in America each year.

I have told the Congress and I have told the nation of the brutal loophole in our nation's laws. Two million guns were sold in the United States last year. Far too many of those guns were bought by the demented and the deranged, the hardened criminal and the convict, the addict and the alcoholic.

And we cannot expect these irresponsible people to be prudent in their protection of us. But we can and we have a right to expect the Congress of the United States to protect us from them.

Weapons of destruction can be purchased by mail as easily as baskets of fruit or cartons of cigarettes.

We must eliminate the dangers of mail-order murder in this country.

The Congress has finally begun to take some action. The Senate has passed a watered-down version of the gun control law I sent to the Congress some time ago with my recommendations.

The House has taken action on the Senate bill. But this halfway measure is not near enough. It covers adequately only transactions involving hand guns. It leaves the deadly commerce in lethal shotguns and rifles without effective control 55 long months after the mailorder murder of President John F. Kennedy.

So today I call upon the Congress in the name of sanity. I call upon the Congress in the name of safety and in the name of an aroused citizenship to give America the gun control law that American citizens need.

I urge the Congress to make it unlawful to sell rifles and shotguns as well as hand guns by mail order. I urge the Congress to make it unlawful to sell rifles and shotguns as well as hand guns to persons who are too young to bear the terrible responsibility that is placed in the hands of a gun owner.

I urge the Congress and plead with it to make it unlawful to sell rifles and shotguns as well as hand guns in one state to the residents of another state.

This will not prevent legitimate hunters or sportsmen from purchasing firearms, but with this reinforced law we can then give the states the proper incentive to shape their own gun control legislation and the country can at long last have a network of systematic safeguards for all of our citizens.

And today I am asking each of the Governors of the 50 states to immediately and to comprehensively review their gun laws and to amend them where necessary and rewrite them in order to fully protect the citizens of the states that they serve, protect them from the deadly weapons that are now in dangerous hands.

The voices of the few must no longer prevail over the interest of the many. When I last appealed to the Congress on this subject again – and that was only a month ago – I asked this question: What in the name of conscience will it take to pass a truly effective gun control law in the Congress.

And now in this new hour of tragedy that question should at last be answered.

So let us now spell out our grief in constructive action.

ON A COMPLETE BOMBING HALT OF NORTH VIETNAM
October 31, 1968

After consultations with the American peace negotiators in Paris, and his military commanders in Vietnam, Johnson ordered a complete halt to the bombing of North Vietnam in order to speed up the peace talks in Paris.

I speak to you this evening about very important developments in our search for peace in Vietnam. We have been engaged in discussions with the North Vietnamese in Paris since last May. The discussions began after I announced on the evening of March 31, in a television speech to the nation, that the United States, in an effort to get talks started on a settlement of the Vietnam war, had stopped the bombing of North Vietnam in the area where 90 per cent of the people live.

When our representatives, Ambassador Harriman and Ambassador Vance, were sent to Paris they were instructed to insist throughout the discussions that the legitimate, elected Government of South Vietnam must take its place in any serious negotiations affecting the future of South Vietnam.

Therefore our Ambassadors Harriman and Vance made it abundantly clear to the representatives of North Vietnam in the beginning that, as I had indicated on the evening of March 31, we would stop the bombing of North Vietnamese territory entirely when that would lead to prompt and productive talks; meaning by that, talks in which the Government of Vietnam was free to participate.

Our Ambassadors also stressed that we could not stop the bombing so long as by doing so we would endanger the lives and the safety of our troops.

For a good many weeks there was no movement in the talks at all. The talks appeared to be really deadlocked. Then a few weeks ago they entered a new and a very much more hopeful phase.

As we moved ahead, I conducted a series of very intensive discussions with our allies and with the senior military and diplomatic officers of the United States Government on the prospects for peace. . . .

Last Sunday evening and throughout Monday we began to get confirmation of the essential understanding that we had been seeking with the North Vietnamese on the critical issues between us for some time.

And I spent most of all day Tuesday reviewing every single detail of this matter with our field commander, General Abrams, whom I had ordered home, and who arrived here at the White House at 2:30 in the morning and went into immediate conference with the President and the appropriate members of his Cabinet. . . .

Now, as a result of all of these developments I have now ordered that all air, naval and artillery bombardment of North Vietnam cease as of 8 A.M. Washington time, Friday morning. I have reaced this decision on the basis of the developments in the Paris talks. And I have reached it in the belief that this action can lead to progress toward a peaceful settlement of the Vietnamese war.

I have already informed the three Presidential candidates, as well as the Congressional leaders of both the Republican and the Democratic parties of the reasons that the Government has made this decision. . . .

It was on Aug. 19 that the President said this Administration does not intend to move further until it has good reasons to believe that the other side intends seriously — seriously — to join us in deescalating the war and moving seriously toward peace.

And then again on Sept. 10, I said the bombing will not stop until we are confident that it will not lead to an increase in American casualties.

The Joint Chiefs of Staff, all military men, have assured me, and General Abrams very firmly asserted to me on Tuesday in that early 2:30 A.M. meeting, that in their military judgment this action would not result in any increase in American casualties.

A regular session of the Paris talks is going to take place on next Wednesday, Nov. 6, at which the representatives of the Government of South Vietnam are free to participate. . . .

The Government of South Vietnam has grown steadily stronger. South Vietnam's armed forces have been substantially increased to the point where a million men are tonight under arms. And the effectiveness of these men has steadily improved.

The superb performance of our men under the brilliant leadership of General Westmoreland and General Abrams has produced truly remarkable results.

Now perhaps some, or all, of these factions played a part in bringing about progress in the talks. And when at last progress did come, I believe that my responsibilities to the brave men, our men, who bear the burden of battle in South Vietnam tonight and my duty to seek an honorable settlement of the war required me to recognize and required me to act without delay.

I have acted tonight.

There have been many long days of waiting for new steps toward peace — days that began in hope, only to end at night in disappointment.

Constancy to our national purpose, which is to seek the basis for a durable peace in Southeast Asia, has sustained me in all of these hours, when there seemed to be no progress whatever in these talks.

But now that progress has come, I know that your prayers are joined with mine and with those of all humanity that the action I announce tonight will be a major step toward a firm and an honorable peace in Southeast Asia. . . .

STATE OF THE UNION ADDRESS
January 14, 1969

Johnson was greeted by a thunderous ovation as he strode to the podium to deliver his final annual message to Congress and the nation. He summed up his administrations in this speech.

For the sixth and the last time, I present to the Congress my assessment of the state of the Union.

I shall speak to you tonight about challenge and opportunity, and about the commitments that all of us have made together that will, if we carry them out, give America our best chance to achieve the kind of a Great Society that we all want. . . .

Urban unrest, poverty, pressures on welfare, education of our people, law enforcement and law and order, the continuing crisis in the Middle East, the conflict in Vietnam, the dangers of nuclear war, the great difficulties of dealing with the Communist powers — all have this much in common:

They and their causes — the causes that gave rise to them — all of these have existed with us for many years. Several Presidents have already sought to try to deal with them. One or more Presidents will try to resolve them or try to contain them in the years that are ahead of us.

But if the nation's problems are continuing, so are this great nation's assets:

Our economy, the democratic system, our sense of exploration symbolized most recently by the wonderful flight of the Apollo 8 in which all Americans took great pride, and the good common sense and sound judgment of the American people and their essential love of justice.

We must not ignore our problems, but neigher should we ignore our strengths. Those strengths are available to sustain a President of either party, to support his progressive efforts both at home and overseas.

Unfortunately, the departure of an Administration does not mean the end of the problems that his Administration has faced. The effort to meet the problems must go on, year after year, if the momentum we have all mounted together in these past years is not to be lost. . . .

Schools and schoolchildren all over America tonight are receiving Federal assistance to go to good schools. And pre-school education — Head Start — is already here to stay. And, I think, so are the Federal programs that tonight are keeping more than a million and a half of our cream of our young people in the colleges and universities of this country.

Part of the American earth − and not only in description on a map, but in the reality of our shores and our hills and our parks and our forests and our mountains − has been permanently set aside for the American public and for their benefit. And there's more going to be set aside before this Administration ends.

Five million Americans have been trained for jobs in new Federal programs. . . .

Tonight the unemployment rate is down to 3.3 per cent. The number of jobs has grown more than 8.5 million in the last five years. And that's more than in all the preceding 12 years.

These achievements completed the full cycle − from idea, from enactment, and finally to a place in the lives of citizens all across this country.

I wish it were possible to say that everything that this Congress and the Administration achieved during this period had already completed that cycle. But a great deal of what we have committed needs additional funding to become a tangible realization. . . .

This much is certain: No one man or group of men made these commitments alone. Congress and the executive branch, with their checks and balances, reasoned together and finally wrote them into the law of the land. And they now have all the moral force that the American political system can summon when it acts as one. . . .

The nation's commitments in the field of civil rights began with the Declaration of Independence. They were extended by the 13th and 14th and 15th Amendments, and they have been powerfully strengthened by the enactment of three far-reaching civil rights laws within the past five years that this Congress in its wisdom passed.

On Jan. 1 of this year, the Fair Housing Act of 1968 covered over 20 million American homes and apartments. The prohibition against racial discrimination in that act should be remembered and it should be vigorously enforced througout this land.

I believe we should also extend the vital provisions of the Voting Rights Act for another five years. . . .

LICENSING OF FIREARMS

Frankly, as I leave the office of the Presidency, one of my greatest disappointments is our failure to secure passage of a licensing and registration act for firearms. I think if we had passed that act it would have reduced the incidence of crime, and, I believe that Congress should adopt such a law, and I hope that it will at a not too distant date. . . .

UNITY WITH WESTERN EUROPE

I think we must continue to support efforts in regional cooperation. Among those efforts, that of Western Europe has a very special place in America's concern. The only course that's going to permit Europe to play the great role, the world role that its resources permit, is to go forward to unity. I think America remains ready to work with the united Europe. Work as a partner on the basis of equality.

For the future, the quest for peace, I believe, requires that we maintain the liberal trade policies that have helped us become the leading nation in world trade; that we strengthen the international monetary system as an instrument of world prosperity, and that we seek areas of agreement with the Soviet Union where the interest of both nations and the interests of world peace are properly served.

The strained relationship between us and the world's leading Communist power has not ended, especially in the light of the brutal invasion of Czechoslovakia.

But totalitarianism is no less odious to us, because we are able to reach some accommodation that reduces the danger of world catastrophe.

What we do, we do in the interest of peace in the world, and we earnestly hope that time will bring a Russia that is less afraid of adversity and individual freedom.

The quest for peace tonight continues in Vietnam and in the Paris talks.

I regret more than any of you know that it has not been possible to restore peace to South Vietnam.

The prospects, I think, for peace are better today than at any time since North Vietnam began its invasion into South Vietnam with its regular forces more than four years ago. . . .

I cannot speak to you tonight about Vietnam without paying a very personal tribute to the men who have carried the battle out there for all of us. And I have been honored to be their Commander-in-Chief. . . .

Finally, the quest for stable peace in the Middle East goes on in many capitals tonight. America fully supports the unanimous resolution of the U.N. Security Council, which points the way.

There must be a settlement of the armed hostilities that exist in that region of the world today. It is a threat not only to Israel, and to all the Arab states, but it's a threat to every one of us and of the entire world as well.

Now my friends in Congress, I want to conclude with a few very personal words to you.

I rejected, and rejected, and then finally accepted the Congressional leadership's invitation to come here to speak this farewell to you in person tonight.

I did that for two reasons. One was philosophical. I wanted to give you my judgment, as I saw it, on some of the issues before our nation, as I view them, before I leave.

The other was just pure sentimental. Most of my life — most all of my life as a public official has been spent here in this building. For 38 years, since I worked in that gallery as a doorkeeper in the House of Representatives, I have known these halls and I have known most of the men pretty well who walked them. I know the questions that you face; I know the conflicts that you endure; I know the ideals that you seek to serve.

CHALLENGES IN OFFICE

I left here first to become the Vice President, and then to become — in a moment of tragedy — the President of the United States. My term of office has been marked by a series of challenges — both at home and throughout the world. In meeting some of these challenges, the nation has found a new confidence. In meeting others, it knew turbulence and doubt, and fear and hate. And throughout this time, I have been sustained by my faith in representative Democracy — a faith that I have learned here in this Capitol Building as an employee and a Congressman and as a Senator.

I believe deeply in the ultimate purposes of this nation — described by the Constitution, tempered by history, embodied in progressive laws, and given life by men and women that have been elected to serve their fellow citizens.

Now, for five most demanding years in the White House I have been strengthened by the counsel and the cooperation of two great former Presidents — Harry S. Truman and Dwight D. Eisenhower.

I have been guided by the memory of my pleasant and close association with the beloved John F. Kennedy, and with our greatest modern legislator — Speaker Sam Rayburn.

I have been assisted by my friend every step of the way — Vice President Hubert Humphrey.

I'm so grateful that I have been supported daily by the loyalty of Speaker McCormack and Majority Leader Albert.

I have benefited from the wisdom of Senator Mike Mansfield. And I am sure that I have avoided many dangerous pitfalls by the good common-sense counsel of the President Pro Tem of the Senate – Senator Richard Brevard Russell.

I have received the most generous cooperation from the leaders of the Republican party in the Congress of the United States – Senator Dirksen and Congressmen Gerald Ford, the minority leader.

No President should ask for more, although I did upon occasion, but few Presidents have ever been blessed with so much. President-elect Nixon, in the days ahead, is going to need your understanding, just as I did, and he is entitled to have it.

And I hope every member will remember that the burdens he will bear as our President will be borne for all of us. Each of us should try not to increase these burdens for the sake of narrow personal or partisan advantage.

And now it's time to leave. I hope it may be said a hundred years from now that by working together we helped to make our country more just – more just for all of its people as well as to insure and guarantee the blessings of liberty for all of our posterity. That's what I hope. But I believe that at least it will be said that we tried.

BIBLIOGRAPHICAL AIDS

Not enough time has passed, nor has sufficient research been done to pass considered judgment on the Administrations of Lyndon B. Johnson. Historians will be analyzing, evaluating, and investigating this period of American history for some time to come. In a meaningful respect, any bibliography or biography of Lyndon Johnson must encompass more than just the five years of his Presidency. His life was so closely intertwined with the workings of American government and politics for such a long time, that in order to come close to understanding the frame of reference that he operated in, one must delve into the operations of American government and politics during the forty years he was in Washington. Therefore, while the purpose of these bibliographical aids is limited, there are, nevertheless, a number of primary sources now available for research. In addition, there is already a considerable amount of secondary material which is casting some light upon the career of this complex and interesting man. Some of the sources are of limited value in researching Johnson's Congressional and Senate periods, and, unfortunately, of even less value in the study of the Presidential period. However, there are large numbers of documents concerned with the Johnson Administrations now available to the public. Speeches, public correspondence, printed reports, private correspondence and mimeographed statements can be found almost anywhere. The Library of Congress contains most of this material, and a considerable portion has already been indexed and microfilmed. In time it is certain that more information will be made available to the researcher and the general public, and that with the completion of the Johnson Library, now under construction on the Texas University campus, a depository of considerable value will be accessible. But, it will be left to future historians to interpret the meaning and importance of Johnson's political career, and especially his years as President.

SOURCE MATERIALS

Congressional Record. Washington, D.C., 1937-1968.

Department of State. *Bulletin.* Washington, D.C., 1961-1968.

Department of State. *Foreign Relations Series,* Washington, D.C., 1961-1968.

Presidential Papers Microfilm: *Lyndon B. Johnson,* 1968-1969.

Public Papers of the Presidents: Lyndon B. Johnson, 1963-1967. 9 vols. Washington, D.C., 1967.

Reports of the Comptroller General of the United States. Washington. D.C., 1948-1968.

Senate Foreign Relations Committee. *Reports.* Washington, D.C., 1963-1968.

BIOGRAPHIES

Amrine, Michael, *This Awesome Challenge; The Hundred Days of Lyndon Johnson.* New York, 1964. Discusses in detail the first three months of Johnson's Presidency, pointing up the difficulties of assuming leadership.

Caidin, Martin, and Hymoff, Edward. *The Mission.* Philadelphia, 1964. This work discusses Johnson's military career, especially his "mission" for President Roosevelt in the South Pacific during World War II.

Davie, Michael. *Lyndon B. Johnson: A Foreign Observer's Viewpoint.* New York, 1967. A highly uncomplimentary biographical sketch of the Johnson Administration by an English journalist.

Evans, Roland, and Novack, Robert. *Lyndon B. Johnson: The Exercise of Power.* New York, 1966. The greater part of this book is given over to Johnson's Senate career, and the operations of the Federal government. Not too complimentary a view.

Goldman, Eric F. *The Tragedy of Lyndon Johnson.* New York, 1969. An outstanding work by an outstanding historian who attempts not only to report the facts of Johnson's career, but also to analyze the strong and weak points of the man.

Mooney, Booth. *The Lyndon Johnson Story.* New York, 1956. A highly partisan view of Johnson's life covering up to his decision to continue as Majority Leader of the Senate following his heart attack.

Newlon Clarke. *LBJ: The Man from Johnson City.* New York, 1964. Rather superficial treatment done in a highly complimentary manner.

Pool, William. *Lyndon Baines Johnson: The Formative Years.* San Marcos, Texas, 1965. Discusses the youth and early career of Johnson. Contains a good deal of valuable information.

Provense, Harry. *Lyndon B. Johnson.* New York, 1964. Good campaign propaganda, but fairly comprehensive as far as it goes. Not many real insights, however.

Robinson, J. A. *The Case for Lyndon Johnson.* New York, 1968. A brilliant and ambitious attempt to defend Johnson's policies, especially his Vietnam decisions.

Sherrill, Robert. *The Accidental President.* New York, 1967. A witty, erudite treatment of the Johnson years written by a journalist who was in Washington during most of the Johnson Administration.

Sidey, Hugh. *A Very Personal Presidency: Lyndon Johnson in the White House.* New York, 1968. This work discusses the day to day operations of the Presidency, and Johnson's influence upon that office.

Singer, Kurt and Jane. *Lyndon Baines Johnson, Man of Reason.* New York, 1964. A rather weak attempt to portray Johnson as a kindly father figure. Some interesting anecdotes.

Steinberg, Alfred. *Sam Johnson's Boy.* New York, 1968. Probably the best biography of Johnson to date. Devastatingly uncomplimentary. Exhaustively researched and brilliantly written.

White, William S. *The Professional: Lyndon B. Johnson.* Boston, 1964. A good, solid biography as far as it goes, although quite laudatory toward Johnson in almost all respects.

Zeiger, Henry. *Lyndon B. Johnson, Man and President.* Boston, 1967. A scholarly account of Johnson's life and work, with both the good and bad points of his career objectively discussed.

Ex-President Johnson is currently engaged in writing his memoirs. Holt-Rinehart-Winston Publishing Company recently announced that they hope to publish the memoirs sometime in 1970.

GENERAL WORKS

These selections, while not strictly biography, deal with Johnson's life, political career, and with various aspects of his years in the White House.

Adler, Bill. *The Johnson Humor.* New York, 1965.

Baker, De Witt Clinton. *A Texas Scrapbook.* New York, 1875.

Baker, Leonard. *The Johnson Eclipse; A President's Vice Presidency.* New York, 1966.

Bell, Jack. *The Johnson Treatment.* New York, 1965.

Bendiner, Robert. *Obstacle Course on Capitol Hill.* New York, 1964.

Bishop, Jim. *A Day in the Life of President Johnson.* New York, 1967.*

Burns, James M. ed. *To Heal and to Build; The Programs of President Lyndon B. Johnson.* New York, 1968.

Clemens, Cyril. *Mark Twain and Lyndon B. Johnson.* Kirkwood, Mo., 1967.

Faber, Harold. ed. *The Road to the White House: The Story of the 1964 Election by the Staff of the New York Times.* New York, 1965.*

Foreign Policy Association. *Great Decisions, 1965.* Washington, D.C., 1965.

_____ *Great Decisions, 1966.* Washington, D.C., 1966.

Gantt, Fred. *The Chief Executive in Texas.* Austin, 1964.

Geyelin, Philip. *Lyndon B. Johnson and the World.* New York, 1966.

Haley, J. Evetts. *A Texan Looks at Lyndon.* Canyon, Texas, 1964.

Johnson, Lyndon B. *A Time For Action, 1953-1964.* New York, 1964.

_____*No Retreat From Tomorrow, President Lyndon B. Johnson's Messages to the Ninetieth Congress.* New York, 1967.

_____*The Promise of New Asia.* Washington, D.C., 1966.

_____*Quotations from Chairman Lyndon B. Johnson,* New York, 1968.

Leighton, Francis. *They Call Her Lady Bird.* New York, 1964.

Lincoln, Evelyn. *Kennedy and Johnson.* New York, 1968.

Montgomery, Ruth. *Mrs. L.B.J.* New York, 1964.

Roberts, Charles. *LBJ's Inner Circle.* New York, 1965.

Rowen, Hobart. *The Free Enterprisers: Kennedy, Johnson, and the Business Establishment.* New York, 1964.

Smith, A. Robert. *The Tiger in the Senate.* New York, 1962.

Smith, Marie. *The President's Lady.* New York, 1964.

Tarr, D. W. *American Strategy in the Nuclear Age.* New York, 1965.*

Weintal, Edward, and Bartlett, Charles. *Facing The Brink.* New York, 1967.

White, Theodore H. *The Making of the President 1960.* New York, 1961.*

———*The Making of the President 1964.* New York, 1965.*

POLITICS AND GOVERNMENT

Adams, Sherman. *First Hand Report.* New York, 1961.

Boykin, Edward. *The Wit and Wisdom of Congress.* New York, 1961.

Brown, Stuart. *Adlai E. Stevenson.* New York, 1965.

Burns, James M. *John Kennedy,* New York, 1959.*

Coffin, Tris. *Senator Fulbright, Portrait of a Public Philosopher,* New York, 1966.

Donovan, Robert. *Eisenhower: The Inside Story.* New York, 1956.

Dorough, C. Dwight. *Mr. Sam.* New York, 1962.

Griffith, Winthrop. *Humphrey.* New York, 1965.

Harris, Joseph. *Advice and Consent of the Senate.* Berkeley, 1952.

Haynes, George. *The Senate of the United States.* 2 vols. Boston, 1938.

Heller, Walter. *New Dimensions of Political Economy.* New York, 1966.

MacDowell, Charles. *Campaign Fever.* New York, 1965.

Manchester, William. *Death of a President.* New York, 1967.*

McKay, Seth. *Texas Politics, 1906-1944.* Lubbock, 1952.

Mollenhoff, Jack. *The Pentagon,* New York, 1967.

Report of the President's Committee on the Assassination of President John F. Kennedy. Washington, D.C., 1964.

Schlesinger, Arthur, Jr. *A Thousand Days.* Boston, 1965.

Strauss, Lewis. *Men and Decisions.* New York, 1962.*

Wicker, Tom. *JFK and LBJ. The Influence of Personality Upon Politics.* New York, 1967.

Weeks, O. D. *Texas Presidential Politics.* Austin, 1953.

Udall, Stewart. *The Quiet Crisis.* New York, 1963.

CIVIL RIGHTS

Baldwin, James. *The Fire Next Time.* New York, 1963.*

Blaustein, Albert P., and Zangrando, Robert L. eds. *Civil Rights and the American Negro.* New York, 1968.*

Broderick, F. L., and Meier, August. eds. *Negro Protest Thought in the Twentieth Century.* New York, 1965.*

Friedman, Leon. Ed. *Southern Justice.* New York, 1965.

King, Martin Luther Jr. *Stride Toward Freedom.* New York, 1958.*

Leinwand, Gerald. ed. *The Negro in the City.* New York, 1968.*

Lewis, Anthony. *Portrait of a Decade.* New York, 1964.

Lincoln, C. Eric. *Black Muslims in America.* New York, 1961.*

Lomax, Louis E. *The Negro Revolt.* New York, 1963.

Lord, Walter. *The Past That Would Not Die.* New York, 1965.

Malcolm X. *Autobiography.* New York, 1966.*

Meredith, James. *Three Years in Mississippi.* New York, 1966.*

Parsons, Talcott, and Clark, Kenneth B. eds. *The Negro in America.* New York, 1966.

Peck, James. *Freedom Ride.* New York, 1962.*

Report of the National Advisory Commission on Cvil Disorders. Washington, D.C., 1968.*

Silberman, Charles E. *Crisis in Black and White.* New York, 1964.*

Silver, James W. *Mississippi: The Closed Society.* (Rev. ed.) New York, 1966.*

Westin, Alan F. ed. *Freedom Now! The Civil Rights Struggle in America.* New York, 1964.

THE WAR ON POVERTY

Caudill, H. M. *Night Comes to the Cumberlands.* New York, 1963.

Fishman, Leo. ed. *Poverty Amid Affluence.* New York, 1966.

Harrington, Michael. *The Other America: Poverty in the United States.* New York, 1963.*

Humphrey, Hubert H. *The War on Poverty.* New York, 1964.

Lewis, Oscar. *La Vida.* New York, 1966.*

Miller, Herman P. *Rich Man, Poor Man.* New York, 1964.

Report of the President's Commission on Appalachia, 1964-1965. Washing-
   ~ton, D.C., 1964-65.

Reports of the Office of Economic Opportunity, 1965-1968. Washington,
   D.C., 1965-68.

Shostak, A. B., and Gomberg, William, eds. *New Perspectives on Poverty.*
   New York, 1966.

THE URBAN CRISIS

Allen, James E. *The Negro in New York,* New York, 1964.*

Drake, St. Clair, and Clayton, Horace R. *Black Metropolis: A Study of
   Negro Life in a Northern City.* New York, 1962.*

Gottmann, Jean. *Megalopolis: The Urbanized Northeast Seaboard of the
   United States.* New York, 1961.*

*Hearings of the Subcommittee on Executive Reorganization of the Com-
   mittee on Government Operation, Federal Committee on Urban
   Affairs.* Washington, D.C., 1966.

Hoover, Edgar M., and Vernon, Raymond. *Anatomy of a Metropolis.*
   New York, 1959.*

Jacobs, Jane. *The Death and Life of Great American Cities.* New York,
   1962.

Katona, George. *The Mass Consumption Society.* New York, 1964.

Pell, Claiborne. *Megalopolis Unbound.* New York, 1966.

Vernon, Raymond. *Metropolis 1985.* New York, 1963.*

Weaver, Robert C. *The Urban Complex.* New York, 1964.*

VIETNAM AND FOREIGN POLICY

Barnett, A. Doak. *Communist China and Asia: A Challenge to American
   Policy.* New York, 1960.*

Browne, Malcolm W. *The Face of War.* Indianapolis, 1965.

Burchett, Wilfred G. *Viet-Nam: Inside Story of the Guerrilla War.* New York, 1965.

Cameron, James. *Here is Your Enemy.* New York, 1966.

Clubb, O. Edmund. *20th Century China.* New York, 1964.

Cole, Allan B., ed. *Conflict in Indo-China and International Repercussions: A Documentary History.* Ithaca, 1956.

Eden, Anthony. *Toward Peace in Indochina.* Boston, 1966.

Fall, Bernard. *Last Reflections on a War.* New York, 1967.

_____*The Two Viet-Nams: A Political and Military History.* New York, 1965.

_____*Viet-Nam Witness 1953-1966.* New York, 1966.

Fulbright, J. William. *The Arrogance of Power.* New York, 1967.

Halberstam, David. *The Making of a Quagmire.* New York, 1965.

Hanh, Thich Nhat. *Vietnam: Lotus in a Sea of Fire.* New York, 1967.

Hillsman, Roger. *To Move a Nation.* New York, 1967.

Honey, P. J. ed. *North Vietnam Today.* New York, 1962.

Kahin, George MCT., and Lewis, John W. *The United States in Vietnam.* New York, 1967.

Kennedy, Robert F. *To Seek a Newer World.* New York, 1967.

Kissinger, Henry, ed. *Problems of National Strategy.* New York, 1965.

La Couture, Jean. *Vietnam Between Two Truces.* New York, 1966.

Martin, John B. *Overtaken by Events.* New York, 1966.

Mecklin, John. *Mission in Torment.* New York, 1965.

Murti, B. S. N. *Vietnam Divided.* New York, 1964.

Pike, Douglas. *Viet Cong: The Organization and Techniques of the National Liberation Front of South Vietnam.* Cambridge, Mass., 1966.

Resichauer, Edwin. *Beyond Vietnam.* New York, 1967.

Schurmann, Franz, Scott, Peter D., and Zelnik, Reginald. *The Politics of Escalation in Vietnam.* New York, 1966.

Scigliano, Robert. *South Vietnam: Nation Under Stress.* Boston, 1963.*

Schlesinger, Arthur Jr. *The Bitter Heritage.* Boston, 1967.*

Taylor, Maxwell. *Responsibility and Response.* New York, 1967.

Trager, Frank. *Why Vietnam?* New York, 1966.*

Zagoria, Donald. *Vietnam Triangle.* New York, 1967.

Zinn, Howard. *The Logic of Withdrawal.* Boston, 1967.

CULTURE AND SOCIETY

Bazelon, David T. *Power in America.* New York, 1967.

Clark, Kenneth B. *Youth in the Ghetto.* New York, 1964.

Cox, Harvey. *The Secular City.* New York, 1966.

Hinkle, Warren. "A Social History of Hippies." *Ramparts.* Vol. 5. No. 9. March, 1967.

Jacobs, Paul, and Landau, Saul. *The New Radicals.* New York, 1966.

Lipset, Seymour M. and Wolin, Sheldon S. *The Berkeley Student Revolt.* New York, 1965.*

McLuhan, Marshall. *The Medium is the Message.* New York, 1967.

Newfield, Jack. *A Prophetic Minority.* New York, 1966.

Toffler, Alvin. *The Culture Consumers.* New York, 1964.

ARTICLES

Alsop, Stewart. "Lyndon Johnson, How He Does It." *Saturday Evening Post.* January 24, 1959.

Carpenter, Leslie. "Whip From Texas." *Collier's.* February 17, 1951.

Cater, Douglass. "Lyndon Johnson, Rising Democratic Star." *Reporter.* January 20, 1953.

Davidson, Bill. "Texas Political Powerhouse." *Look.* August 4, 1959.

Harrison, Selig. "Lyndon Johnson's World." *New Republic.* June 13, 1960.

King, Harry. "My Hero: LBJ." *Harper's.* October, 1966.

Sidey, Hugh. "Measure of a Man." *Life.* December 3, 1965.

Steinberg, Alfred. "GAO: The Taxpayer's Best Friend." *Reader's Digest.* November, 1967.

Anonymous. "Down on the Ranch, Hospitality to Washington Press Corps." *Time.* January 17, 1964.

Wicker, Tom. "Lyndon Johnson is Ten Feet Tall." *New York Times Magazine.* May 23, 1965.

NAME INDEX